## PRAISE FOR 10 WAYS ANYONE CAN GRADUATE FROM COLLEGE DEBT-FREE

*"I decided to enroll in Debt Free College Academy's Full Course program. The value for the money was absolutely amazing."* - **Diane M., Debt Free College Academy Graduate and Parent**

*"I would recommend this program to anybody"* - **Kelly D., Debt Free College Academy Graduate and Parent**

*"If I didn't use the strategies in the book 10 Ways Anyone Can Graduate College Debt Free, I would be walking out of College with $160,000 in debt."* - **Joshua F., College student**

*"Well thought out strategies that can be used by any student and their parents as they navigate through the college financial aid maze."* - **Fred D. Mitchell, Vice President, Development United Negro College Fund**

*"Kevin Y. Brown takes his personal decisions and experiences and creates a guidebook for any student who seriously wants a college education but does not have the means to afford it."* - **Dr. Carlton E. Brown, President, Clark Atlanta University 2008-2015**

*"I thought the book was just going to be about scholarships available for youth... I read his book and highly recommend it to any student who is going into college and any adult who is encouraging students going to college. I was impressed with every part of it.* - **Nancy Horn, Educational Liason Fresno Unified School District**

*"Kevin Brown has done a phenomenal job and this book will change your life"* - **Les Brown, World renown Speaker and Author**



www.debtfreecollegeacademy.com

Twitter: @KevinYBrown | Facebook.com/KevBrown001

# 10 WAYS ANYONE CAN GRADUATE FROM COLLEGE DEBT-FREE

---

# 2.0

*A Guide to Post-College Freedom*

KEVIN Y. BROWN

www.debtfreecollegeacademy.com

# 10 WAYS ANYONE CAN GRADUATE FROM COLLEGE DEBT-FREE
# 2.0

-

*A Guide to Post-College Freedom*

by KEVIN Y. BROWN



ISBN: 978-0-9847671-2-0 (EPub)
ISBN: 978-0-9847671-3-7 (Paperback)

Twitter: @KevinYBrown | Facebook.com/KevBrown001

## ATTENTION: SCHOOLS, ORGANIZATIONS AND CORPORATIONS

This book serves as the textbook for our online programs and 91-day Debt Free College in class curriculum. This book and our online programs are available at special quantity discounts for bulk purchases for sales promotions, premiums, or fund raising. For more information, please contact us at admin@LegacyThinkingLabs.com or (347) 871 - 8273

www.debtfreecollegeacademy.com

# SEMINARS BY KEVIN Y. BROWN

Debt - Free College 101

Create Your Life!

Molding A Brand

Diversity U

Meet Kevin online and receive free college financial training at

**www.debtfreecollegeacademy.com**

Twitter: @KevinYBrown | Facebook.com/KevBrown001

# DEDICATION

This book is dedicated to Mr. Philmore Graham and Mrs. Carrie S. Wilson—two people who changed the course of my life by exposing me to the value of education and holding me to higher standards.

AND

My dearest Marie Elizabeth Dutton Brown—without you, this project would not have been possible.

*THANK YOU FOR EVERYTHING!!!*

Twitter: @KevinYBrown | Facebook.com/KevBrown001

# CONTENTS

***Note: All statistics are 100% accurate and current at the time of publication. Because information is continually being updated we recommend that readers research our sources as well as others in order to find the most recent data.*

Twitter: @KevinYBrown | Facebook.com/KevBrown001

# 10 Ways Anyone Can Graduate From College DEBT-FREE

"If I have to take out a loan for college, I'm dropping out!" is what I said to my dormitory hall director, Dr. Raphael X. Moffett, a few days into college. This comment was my response during a conversation that we were having about students' struggles to obtain loans and the possibility that they would be sent home because they could not meet their financial obligation.

When I said that I would drop out if I had to take out a loan for college, my hall director and the other students looked at me as if I was crazy and sarcastically wished me good luck. Dr. Moffett told me that most of the students had student loans. I quickly repeated, "I don't care; If I have to take out a loan for college, I'm dropping out." I kept that promise to myself and today I am student loan debt-free.

I have written this book because I now have an unusual freedom that most of my peers who attended college do not. That freedom is a result of zero college debt. Although my peers may earn good salaries, a considerable amount of their money goes toward repaying college loans, and they frequently tell me how much they wish they had searched for scholarships and grants while in school.

While they are stressed out about their student loan debt, I have had the opportunity to move to New York—one of the most expensive cities in the world—without having to take a job I did not want in order to repay a loan. What is even better is that my debt-free college experience has allowed me to run my own business while traveling abroad to places such as England, Iceland, Jamaica, Mexico, Spain, Rome, Egypt, Japan, South Africa and Australia.

I'm not saying this to brag; I am telling you this so that you can visualize what working hard to find free money for your college education can offer you versus being trapped in a job, city, or country for the next thirty years because of your student loan debt. I don't worry about the burden of monthly payments to a lender, or avoiding annoying phone calls from agencies trying to collect money from me. Truthfully, I don't want you to either, because repaying student loans can become overwhelming.

The pressure of student loan debt makes it almost impossible not to scramble to find a job as soon as you graduate. And it also increases your possibility of accepting an undesirable job that simply pays your bills. While in college, the majority of students you encounter will accept loans as the method of financing their college educations. Don't follow their lead.

By following the strategies outlined in this book, you will obtain the tools needed to fund a free college education and discover the freedom of graduating debt-free.

# Why 10 Ways Anyone Can Graduate From College DEBT-FREE Is For YOU!

10 Ways Anyone Can Graduate From College DEBT-FREE is written from experience. In the chapters that follow, you will find my story and the strategies that make my statement, "If I have to take out a loan, I'm dropping out!" true.

To assure you that a free college-level education is possible, I have listed the following challenges that I faced before entering college, and the subsequent results that I achieved with the ten strategies offered in this book:

**CHALLENGES**

- I was raised in California's foster care system for seventeen years
- I grew up in one of the worst neighborhoods in Northern California: The Country Club Crest in Vallejo
- I scored in the $40^{th}$ percentile on my SAT
- I had minimal financial support from family and friends
- I was the first in my biological and immediate foster care families to leave the state to attend a university
- I had no knowledge of the college financing system
- Because of my attitude and behavioral history, my mentors and foster parents expected me to be kicked out of college within my first week.

## RESULTS AFTER IMPLEMENTING THE STRATEGIES OUTLINED IN THIS BOOK

- I double-majored in Fashion Design/Merchandising and Business Supply Chain Management
- I spent a semester abroad in London, England
- I graduated with 178 credit hours
- I was financially able to travel back and forth to California (and other states) for school vacations
- I played for Clark Atlanta University's men's basketball team
- **I obtained a FREE five-year college education valued at over $140,000!**

Considering the challenges I was faced with, if I graduated college debt-free, then you can too!

# THE VALUE OF HIGHER EDUCATION:
## *Education vs. Income*

Higher education is invaluable. Many skill-building, networking, and training opportunities are available on college campuses. Professional skill-building workshops offered on-campus are offered by major corporations, and students in leadership groups, clubs, or on athletic teams are recruited. Some of these programs are as basic as proper dining etiquette and networking with other professionals. Students often benefit from attending banquets, dinners, and events where decision-makers and sponsors are present. You can find these programs off-campus, but those who attend on-campus events will often have a higher education profile, which can make networking more beneficial.

Higher education places you within a network of people who could be tomorrow's leaders; those individuals who are striving to attain similar goals to yours offer you access to more resources than most. It also teaches you critical thinking skills and how to be culturally competent to compete in today's diverse world. I had teammates and other college friends from foreign countries such as Ghana, France, and Jamaica to name a few. Our friendships allowed me greater insight into lifestyles in places around the globe, which prepared me for my study abroad experience in London. There, I learned even more about other cultures and ways of life.

A higher education provides you with the skill set to compete with others all over the world and makes moving into management, changing jobs, or entering higher-level jobs much easier. For example, I often hear of stories about where a person has been working at a job for twenty years and applies for a management position only to lose the job to someone with a higher education who has no experience. This is not always the case but often, a degree is comparable to experience and says that a person with a higher education can handle a job because they have been taught to think critically. Hiring a person with higher education can boost the credibility of a company.

Higher education is not limited to four-year colleges. Concentrated programs, two-year degrees and other forms of training all constitute as higher education. While having a diverse background and diverse life experiences can boost the credibility of your resume, higher education is one of the most universal ways to move up financially in society.

The higher your education level, the more likely you are to be employed when the economy is in an economic downturn. Your education level affects the amount of money you can earn in your lifetime. As a high school graduate, I would earn a little over $1 million dollars in my lifetime. The *Median Synthetic Work-Life Earnings table* below shows the lifetime earnings of Americans according to their education level. This table is available for download when you sign up for your free $1 Million dollar scholarship list at **www.debtfreecollegeacademy.com/free.**

MEDIAN SYNTHETIC WORK- LIFE EARNINGS

| EDUCATION LEVEL | 2015 UNEMPLOYMENT RATES (%) | 2015 WEEKLY WAGES/SALARY | 2015 ANNUAL WAGES/SALARY | WORK LIFE EARNINGS* |
|---|---|---|---|---|
| LESS THAN A HIGH SCHOOL DIPLOMA | 1.7 | $493 | $25,636 | $1,025,440 |
| HIGH SCHOOL DIPLOMA | 1.5 | $678 | $35,256 | $1,410,240 |
| SOME COLLEGE (BUT NO DEGREE) | 2.4 | $738 | $38,376 | $1,535,040 |
| ASSOCIATE DEGREE | 2.8 | $798 | $41,496 | $1,659,840 |
| BACHELOR'S DEGREE | 3.8 | $1,137 | $59,124 | $2,364,960 |
| MASTER'S DEGREE | 5.0 | $1,341 | $69,732 | $2,789,280 |
| PROFESSIONAL DEGREE | 5.4 | $1,730 | $89,960 | $3,598,400 |
| DOCTORAL DEGREE | 8.0 | $1,623 | $84,396 | $3,375,840 |

***Table 1 Median Synthetic Work-Life Earnings***
Note: Data are for persons age 25 and over. Earnings are for full-time wage and salary workers.

*Source: Bureau of Labor Statistics U.S. Department of Labor, 2016. "Earnings and unemployment rates by educational attainment Table: ep_table_001" http://www.bls.gov/emp/ep_table_001.htm*

**The Numbers are based on averages and do not reflect the financial reality for every person in the United States of America. People may make more or less.*

# STUDENT LOAN DEBT AT A GLANCE

Student loan debt is borrowed money plus accumulated interest that is owed to lenders. According to debt.org a student accrues $3,000 in student loan debt every second while graduating with an average of $37,172[1] in student loan debt. The total amount of student loan debt is now 1.3 trillion dollars and rising[2]. Nationally, student loan debt is higher than both credit card and auto loan debt.

Many students and parents take student loans as their primary method of financing a college education because they cannot pay out of pocket or are unaware of other financing options such as grants, scholarships, or fellowships that may be available.

Some students and parents take on student loans because they find it easier to apply for a loan than complete the work that is required to apply for a scholarship. A loan can also be seen as a source of guaranteed money that most college students are using, while scholarships are seen as an opportunity to win the money to finance expenses. Sometimes, students may not have the grades to compete for merit-based aid, but it is still important to be aware of what your options are and understand that there are various methods to finance your college education without loans.

By signing up on the books website at **www.debtfreecollegeacademy.com/free**, you gain access to a $1 million dollar scholarship list and here is a little motivation to apply for the scholarships: student loan interest results in a borrower repaying lenders more than his or her initial loan. Use your coupon code **DFCA10** for a 10% discount on your Debt Free College online course.

---

[1] DiGangi, Christine. "The Class of 2016 Will Graduate With an Average of $37,172 in Debt." *Time* 5.

[2] The Institute for College Access & Success. 2014. Quick Facts about Student Debt. http://bit.ly/1QcRwmn

**More Student Loan Debt Facts:**

- 43.3 million Americans have student loan debt[3]

The Institute for College Access & Success has provided additional information about American student loan debt:

- In 2012, 71 percent of students graduating from four-year colleges had student loan debt.
- 1.3 million students graduating with debt, an increase from 1.1 million in 2008
- 66 percent of graduates from public colleges had loans (average debt of $25,550)
- 75 percent of graduates from private nonprofit colleges had loans (average debt of $32,300)
- 88 percent of graduates from for-profit colleges had loans (average debt of $39,950)
- Graduates who received Pell Grants were likely to borrow more:
- 88 percent of graduates who received Pell Grants had student loans in 2012, with an average balance of $31,200
- 53 percent of those who didn't receive a Pell Grant had student loan debt and borrowed $4,750 less ($26,450)[4]

More than $200 billion is owed in government student loans, raising worries that millions of them may never repay because 40% of Americans who borrowed are behind on payments..[5]

---

[3] Source: Andrew Haughwout, Donghoon Lee, Joelle Scally, Wilbert van der Klaauw. "Student Loan Borrowing and Repayment Trends." Federal Reserve Bank of New York 16. April. 2015. Web. 18 June. 2016. <https://www.newyorkfed.org/medialibrary/media/newsevents/mediaadvisory/2015/Student-Loan-Press-Briefing-Presentation.pdf>

[4] *Source: The Institute for College Access & Success. 2014. Quick Facts about Student Debt. http://bit.ly/1QcRwmn*

[5] Mitchell, Josh. "More Than 40% of Student Borrowers Aren't Making Payments." *Wallstreet Journal* 7. April. 2016. Web. 19 June. 2016. <http://www.wsj.com/articles/more-than-40-of-student-borrowers-arent-making-payments-1459971348>

Although over two-thirds of college students have accumulated federal and private loans, you don't have to follow the majority. In this book, you have the power and the tools to be the exception to the student loan debt rule. You also have the option to take what you learn in this book much further in our online courses at **www.debtfreecollegeacademy.com/programs.** Our online courses offer you in-depth actual information and a skillset that provides many advantages that support unique learning methods such as auditory, kinesthetic and/or visual.

# CONSEQUENCES of DEFAULTING on STUDENT LOANS

Obtaining student loan debt can have severe consequences if you are not responsible with money or don't repay your debts on time. According to www.finaid.org, student loan default happens when a borrower has failed to make payments on his or her federal student loans for 270-360 days and does not make special arrangements with their lender to get a deferment or forbearance (postponement of payment on a loan).

The reasons why a loan can go into default can vary, but the most common causes are unemployment and a person's financial mismanagement. In these instances, borrowers can set up monthly payment plans with loan lenders based upon their monthly income.

Failing to pay your student loans on time, also known as defaulting, can lead to severe and frustrating consequences. Below are nine penalties that you can be subjected to if you default on your loans:[6]

1. **Administrative Wage Garnishment**
   If you do not voluntarily make arrangements to repay your student loan(s), up to 15% of your pay check can be taken by federal or private loan lenders without your consent.

2. **Collection Costs**
   When you sign your promissory note before receiving your loan(s), you agree to repay your student loan lender. If you default on your loan(s), the outstanding amount will be sent to a collection agency and you will have to pay the cost for the agency collecting on your debt, which can be added to the total balance of your loan. The rates for collection costs are re-

---

6 *"Consequences of Student Loan Default." TG Online. Texas Guaranteed Student Loan Corporation, 15 Sept. 2011. Web. 22 Oct. 2011.*

calculated annually and the percentage rate is subject to change due to administrative costs, or the assignment of your account to other collection agencies. Keep in mind that the adjustment in your rate can increase or decrease your total balance due.

3. **License Suspension**
   There are many states that allow professional and vocational boards to refuse to certify, certify with restrictions, suspend, or revoke a member's professional or vocational license. In some cases, states allow professional and vocational boards to impose fines on members if they default on their student loans. License suspensions are applicable to the legal, healthcare, teaching, insurance, state, and commercial fishing professions.[7]

4. **Credit Reporting**
   TransUnion, Experian, and Equifax are the three credit bureaus that can be notified of the original amount and current balance of each of the student loans that you default on. A loan(s) in default will continue to show up on your credit report for seven consecutive years after the original date of delinquency.

5. **Reinstatement of Eligibility for Federal Student Aid**
   Once a student loan is declared in default, you no longer have the option for deferments or forbearances. In addition, you cannot receive any additional Title IV* federal student aid until you have made approved payments for a minimum of six consecutive months.

6. **Withholding of Transcripts and Academic Records**
   Each school has its individual policy for releasing academic records. Some schools may require additional documentation or verification of your current repayment status before

---

[7] *"License Revocations | Student Loan Borrower Assistance." Student Loan Borrower Assistance | A Resource for Borrowers, Their Families and Advocates. National Consumer Law Center. Web. 22 Oct. 2011.*

releasing academic records such as enrollment/attendance records, academic transcripts, certificates, degrees, etc.

7. **Treasury Offset Program**
   When you are eligible to receive a federal tax refund from the federal government, this money can be garnished to repay your defaulted student loan(s).

8. **You Can Be Sued**
   The government and private lenders can sue you to collect up to the entire amount of your student loan(s). There are no time limits on when the government and private lenders can sue you to collect student loan debt.

9. **Your Federal Benefits Can Be Taken**
   The government can garnish your federal benefit payments (Social Security and Social Security Disability benefits (SSDI)) as reimbursement for any student loan that you default on. These benefit garnishments exclude Supplemental Security Income (SSI) and can be executed without a statute of limitations. (Lockhart v. U.S. (04-881) 546 U.S. 142 (2005)

Consider and use these penalties as your motivation to research and apply for scholarships and grants in order to avoid the headaches of repaying student loans.

**Title IV funds include all federal financial aid program funds. Examples are: Pell Grant, Federal Supplemental Educational Opportunity Grants (FSEOG), Academic Competitiveness Grants (ACG), National Science and Mathematics Access to Retain Talent (National SMART), Teacher Education Assistance for College and Higher Education Grants (TEACH), Leveraging Educational Assistance Partnership (LEAP) and Special LEAP (SLEAP) Grants, Direct Loan Program, Federal Perkins Loans, Work-Study)*

# TYPES OF FINANCIAL AID

Financial Aid is funding given to students by the government for educational expenses including tuition, books, room and board. There are two types of financial aid: 1) merit-based and 2) Need-based.

**Merit-Based Aid:** Financial aid that anyone can receive no matter his or her level of need.

Merit-based financial aid is free money that comes in the form of scholarships. These can be awarded to students by any college, university, or outside organization for special talents, outstanding academic achievements, or leadership potential. In some cases, scholarships are renewable.

**Need-Based Aid:** Financial aid based on your needs.

Need-based aid requires that a form, The Free Application for Federal Student Aid (FAFSA), be filled out by both undergraduate and graduate students in the United States to determine their eligibility for loans, federal and state grants, and work-study programs.

**Loans** are funds borrowed to pay for college expenses that **must be repaid** with interest to lenders. There are five types of federal loans:

- Federal Perkins Loan
- Federal Stafford Loan
- PLUS Loan for Parents
- PLUS Loan for Graduate and Professional Degree Students
- Consolidation Loan

**Grants** are funds disbursed by the state and federal government that **do not have to be repaid**. There are four types of grants:

- Federal Pell Grant
- Federal Supplemental Educational Opportunity Grant (FSEOG)

- Teacher Education Assistance for College and Higher Education (TEACH) Grant
- Iraq and Afghanistan Service Grants

**Work-Study** is a federal student job program that allows students to earn money while enrolled in college to help fund their educational expenses.

**Scholarships** are funds that do not have to be repaid. Scholarships can be athletic or academic-based and are disbursed through your college/university, a fraternity, sorority, alumni association, or through many other sources inside and outside of your campus community.

This next section entails the strategies which I personally used to graduate college debt-free. When you read beyond this point you are making up your mind that you are going to give your DEBT-FREE college journey all you have. GO FOR IT!

# 10 WAYS ANYONE CAN GRADUATE FROM COLLEGE DEBT-FREE

---

# 2.0

www.debtfreecollegeacademy.com

STRATEGY

# 1

# EXCEL IN HIGH SCHOOL

Attending school for seven or more hours a day and squeezing in time to hang out with friends can sometimes blur your connection between high school and college. Yes, college is definitely an enjoyable place to be, but your academic performance, conduct, and extra-curricular activities in high school can dictate to which colleges you get accepted, and can also affect the type of college experience you have. When your high school transcript reflects high grades, an upward trend in higher grades, and/or honor classes, you will receive more college acceptances and more college scholarships.

While in high school, I was disciplined, made an effort to earn good grades, and developed good study habits. As a result of my hard work, Clark Atlanta University (CAU) paid me to attend.

Good academic performance may often help you avoid the consequences of any bad conduct. However, once you reach a certain age and are in certain academic environments, your conduct is expected to reflect your capability. This is a time when it no longer pays to be the bad boy or girl. You will be competing with others who do not hide their intelligence with foolish behavior. In fact, you may find that while many of your peers are not as smart as you, they know how to conduct themselves in a way that gives the impression that they are top performing students. Sometimes this is accomplished by being quiet or saying less than everyone else. In short, it pays to act as smart as you are.

If you are anything like I was and are not too familiar with how to conduct yourself in certain environments, it may be in your best interest to become involved in positive extra-curricular activities. Often, these are the places where you can observe many kids and parents who know how to conduct themselves, and they can assist you.

Although excelling in high school is one of the smartest ways to earn a free college education, it may not always be the easiest. There are many distractions such as girls, boys, social media and peer pressure, but keep in mind that your main job is to focus on your grades. It's required by law that you attend high school, so you might as well do your best. You may not see it now, but your conduct and academic performance in high school will impact your life well after you graduate.

Becoming an A/B student may not be easy for everyone, and that's okay. Keep in mind that just because a course is challenging, it doesn't make it impossible to attain good grades. Whether you are taking Honor or Advanced Placement (AP) courses, or studying for countless hours, tutoring and homework resources are available.

Seeking help from a tutor is highly recommended. Think of tutors as coaches or mentors. What professional dancer, athlete, or musician do you know who doesn't have a coach to help them improve their skills? A tutor is a teacher. If you do not have a coach/tutor to help you improve your skills, then you are not really trying to be the best that you can be. You are maximizing your potential by asking for help. Those subjects that you may be struggling with now could be beneficial in the future.

You can maximize your potential by maintaining a high grade point average (GPA). Hanging out with friends whose goals are to be successful and productive can expand your experiences as well as open doors for you that otherwise might be closed. For example, participation in leadership classes, honor societies, social clubs, athletics, and community service activities can help others and build your network and character. Although some extra-curricular activities do not require a minimum GPA, you can always use your academic GPA to gain access to anything you want; your GPA and conduct are your passports to new places and opportunities. Positive and productive extra-curricular activities are where most of your peers who are focused on being their best and having great futures will be. It is exciting to surprise people with your high GPA. The look of approval on their faces is always priceless.

The scholarship application process can be time-consuming but the preparation for this and your college education begins in high school. Developing your reputation, academic and extra-curricular activity performance are important elements in maximizing scholarship opportunities and your college experience. It could mean the difference between repaying student loans and a debt-free post-college life!

Another option is to consider earning your associate degree from a community college and high school diploma at the same time. I recommend this for any student who is extremely focused and has the discipline to balance the two objectives. By accomplishing this goal, you will enter college as a junior at 18 years old, which means that you can obtain your bachelors by 20 and if you choose to continue your education eventually earning either a masters or juris doctor degree (law) by the time you are 23.

***Author's Experiences and Opinions:***

- *Various opportunities and a positive circle of peers can provide you with access to information, people, and experiences that can propel you to the next level. Below is an example of how hanging out with a positive friend took me to a higher level.*

  *In high school, I lived in one of the worst neighborhoods in Vallejo, California, but no one could tell by looking at my transcript. My teachers, principal, and athletic coaches were all aware of my academic capabilities, but they were also aware of my poor behavior. I needed to make some changes, so I joined the leadership class, began to volunteer in school and the surrounding communities, and created new and positive relationships with other kids who were doing positive things and achieving their goals.*

  *Ironically, most of the other kids who were doing well and preparing for their future happened to be from the other part of town far from my neighborhood. As our friendships grew stronger, I began to see more of what life was like from their perspective, as well as their parents'. They invited me to their nice homes, where there were bigger TVs, better food than I ate at home, lots of books, and a peaceful environment. Their conversations were frequently centered on future life plans and goals; they knew leaders in the city who had access to scholarships, and also knew which colleges were best to attend.*

  *Generally, there were more constructive things to do at their houses. Activities that I considered a privilege, such as going into the refrigerator whenever I wanted, cooking whatever I liked, using the family car, or conversing about a difference of opinion with parents, were activities that my friends considered normal. My experience with different friends, their families, and the observations of their households inspired me to want more out of life. It also granted me more access to gatekeepers: people who could improve my circumstances by giving me important information for scholarships and other tools that I needed to excel.*

*When administrators and teachers saw me running errands or helping with activities for other staff members, they made a mental note of it. If they didn't, I reminded them. And that helped me to access scholarship information, free transcripts, administrative assistance, and other privileges.*

- *By maneuvering intelligently through high school e.g. making friends with those in charge and their secretaries, and spending your time with people who are constantly striving for brighter futures, your high school community will be supportive. They will consider you one of their own. They'll want to push you to excel so that you can be one of their success stories. Why? Because it makes what they do more meaningful.*

- *The great thing about applying for scholarships while in high school is that you can accumulate several scholarships to pay for college expenses prior to enrollment. For example, I applied for and received a $2,000 General Mills scholarship during my junior year of high school. Then, after participating in the Boys and Girls Club and volunteering in the community and maintaining a 3.0 GPA, I re-applied during senior year and won the same amount. This gave me a total of $4,000 to use toward college tuition and textbooks before I began my freshman year of college.*

- *Preparation for your free college education begins in high school; the habits that you develop will carry over into college. Excel in high school so that you are prepared to excel in college.*

STRATEGY

# 2

# SACRIFICE

Whenever focusing time and energy into achieving a goal, such as obtaining a scholarship or 4.0 GPA, you may find yourself sacrificing another activity or desire. Each sacrifice has its challenges and some may make you question the purpose of your goal. When this occurs, embrace it and think about the bigger picture in order to understand why you are making the sacrifice.

Achieving a debt-free college education will come with many challenges, but you can overcome them to achieve the following:

- The freedom to travel and live anywhere you want after college without limiting your options due to accumulated student loan debt.
- The ability to begin saving or achieving your desires with your earnings after college instead of repaying lenders.

Four sacrifices that you may have to endure on your debt-free college journey:

- **Time at Home** – Realize that life-changing events such as births, deaths, health issues of family and friends, etc. occur during your college years.
- **Social Time** – Partying and hanging out with friends.
- **Luxury Lifestyle** – Extra spending money, nice clothes, dining out, etc.
- **Immediate Gratification** – You will do the hard work (applying for scholarships, getting good grades, and making the right connections) up front to reap the benefits of not having to repay college loans.

While in college, you may spend more time away from home than you ever have. During this time, whether days, hours, or months, things at home will change. New people will move into your neighborhood, childhood friends may move away, or a family member's health may improve or worsen, and others may even die. You may be there to witness these events, or you may be away working towards a better future for yourself and your family.

It is very important at times like these to separate your goals from what is happening at home. So often, this is a very difficult decision, but the time that you spend on assignments, improving your work ethic, or networking, can mean the difference between being financially stable after college or not.

While in college, the grass may seem greener for those who chose not to attend because they will often have access to money, cars, clothes, and a lifestyle that may be attractive to you at the moment. This may cause you to ask yourself, *why am I studying and broke when I can have things that others have now?* You must answer this question by telling yourself that you are working to place yourself in a position to be able to have a lifestyle better than what you are currently witnessing.

Pursuing a debt-free college education might be one of the poorest times in your life, but I can assure you that if you stay the course and complete your DEBT-FREE college education, there are strong possibilities that you will have all of the things that you desire and so much more—including priceless experiences that will bring you friends who share your same ambitions in life. College is one of the best sacrifices I have ever made and I loved it so much that I would do it all over again.

Another necessary sacrifice in order to achieve a debt-free college education is balancing your time. If your peers are financing their education with student loans then they appear financially stable for the time being, but remember that they must begin repaying the money they borrowed (with interest) six months after graduation. Over the years, the amount initially borrowed can double or triple. To reach your debt-free college goal, you must work harder than other students, maintain a high average, constantly research scholarships, and network with influential people while your peers may be hanging out, taking trips, or relaxing.

Each student's schedule and priorities will vary according to personal preferences. You may have to sacrifice hanging out and sleeping-in to work toward your post-college freedom. You will have to decide whether to chill, hangout and take the loans offered to you. I suggest making the sacrifice to work hard up front. While it took a lot of dedication and balance, I definitely had fun while working hard on my DEBT-FREE college journey, and you can too; it just takes balance. (See Strategy 7: Master Your Schedule.)

Yes, you will miss out on some parties, relaxation, and sleep, but those who work hard are barely seen because they are always working, and this can make their presence more valuable. Have you ever heard the phrase *absence makes the heart grow fonder*, which suggests that people miss you more when you are not around? This fact is one reason why the paparazzi get paid so much for photographs of celebrities who happen to be some of the hardest working and successful people. The paparazzi get paid because it is hard to see celebrities everywhere. Missing some events and being inaccessible at times can cause others to be more interested in what you are up to. Being unavailable to hang out and missing social events due to working to become your best is the norm for the top achievers in every profession.

If you sacrifice a little bit of relaxation and play time, you will be able to save your money in order to build your wealth after college.

Sacrifice also means understanding delayed gratification, which is sacrificing something up front to receive the benefits of your sacrifice later. You will be faced with decisions that will require sacrifice continuously throughout your college days. Often, your sacrifice will be related to the topics mentioned at the beginning of this chapter: time at home, social time, luxury lifestyle and immediate gratification. When faced with these decisions you must try to do what will serve you best overall and enable you to reach your goals. There will always be another party or time to relax but you have four to five key years to make decisions that can save you headaches and assure your financial freedom after college.

Many say a DEBT-FREE college education is impossible, but I stand with a select group of people who can tell you from experience that it is very possible. The decision is yours to make.

One of the best ways to keep sight of your DEBT-FREE college education goal is to completely understand why you are willing to work toward the goal. To do so, complete a "Why Sacrifice" worksheet, which will allow you to visualize and anticipate the challenges, sacrifices, and pros and cons of obtaining your debt-free college education. The following is an example of what a completed "Why Sacrifice" worksheet looks like.

## WHY SACRIFICE WORKSHEET

**My goal:** To graduate college debt-free

**My anticipated sacrifices:**

1. Partying and hanging out as much as everyone else
2. New clothes
3. Time at home
4. Dining out
5. Trips and vacations

**Why I am willing to make these sacrifices:**

1. Because I want to be free to do what I want after I graduate
2. Because I want to keep the money I earn
3. Because I do not want to take out student loans and have to repay lenders
4. Because when I graduate I want to be able to immediately help my family financially without hindering myself

**Pros of achieving my goal:**

1. I will be a college graduate
2. I can make more money than I typically would without a degree
3. This is a milestone
4. I will not owe any student loan vendors any money
5. I will have post-college freedom
6. I am free to travel and do as I wish because I don't have any debt and I don't have to take the first job offered to me
7. I will be stress free

**Cons of not achieving my goal:**

1. I will graduate college, but I'll have to begin to repay loan lenders six months after I graduate
2. I may have to take any job I can get just to start paying back my debt
3. I may experience high levels of stress trying to figure out how to pay back student loans
4. I may be in debt for the rest of my life due to the interest rates on my loans and how long it takes me to repay them.

Your "Why Sacrifice" worksheet is very important and I suggest keeping it in a safe place so that you can look at it whenever you feel that you cannot achieve your goal because of its challenges. I used this technique to keep my eye on my DEBT-FREE college prize and the cool thing is that it helped me to accomplish other goals in addition to my debt-free college education.

To help reach your debt-free college goal, download the "Why Sacrifice" worksheet when you sign up for your free $1 million dollar scholarship list on our website **www.debtfreecollegeacademy.com/free**

***<u>Author's Experiences and Opinions:</u>***

- *Sacrificing time at home is something that comes with the territory of achievement. Many things changed when I was in college over 2,000 miles away from home. Jeremiah, my oldest nephew, was growing up and I only saw him during Christmas breaks or summer vacations. I missed some of his early years because graduating college debt-free was my number one priority.*

  *Also, while I was away in college, two of my friends died and I wasn't able to attend their funerals. Some family members became sick while others recovered from serious illnesses; one of my mentors lost his memory, and a few of my friends were starting families and businesses.*

  *During these times of sorrow and happiness, I had to stay focused in order to stay committed to my goal of graduating college debt-free. It was a huge sacrifice to miss so much while being away. Who knows where I would be if I weren't away in college focused on my future? The sacrifice of being away from home also taught me that my family and friends would survive while I was away. When things became really challenging for me I used my "Why Sacrifice" list to stay focused.*

- *There is always the opportunity to study abroad while in college and leaving the country can be a hard decision. I thought long and hard before I left for London for a quarter. My decision to study abroad placed me over 5,400 miles from my family and hometown, but the experience was more than worth it.*

- *During my junior year of college, I had to make a really tough decision. I was a fashion design major and every year during my college's homecoming week, the fashion department assisted in the production of a fashion show. This show was a big deal and very instrumental in a fashion student's understanding of fashion show production. Fashion majors also received credit for participating.*

  *During one of our practices, my basketball coach told the team that if any of us missed practice because of the homecoming fashion show, we would be kicked off of the team. He was still upset from the previous season because one of the players missed practice to model in the fashion show. After practice, I went to speak with my coach to plead my case. I told him that I would have to miss practice for the fashion show because it was a part of my curriculum as a fashion design major. He responded by telling me that he meant what he said: If anyone misses practice because of the homecoming fashion show they are going to be kicked off of the team. No exceptions. I discussed the matter with my coach a few more times and even spoke with the assistant coaches to try to get him to change his mind, but he wouldn't budge.*

  *Finally, the day of the fashion show came, and I had to make a decision. Something was going to be sacrificed. I remember thinking to myself; do I sacrifice my grades or my athletic scholarship that I worked two years to earn? I reflected on what I was taught growing up in the Continentals of Omega Boys and Girls Club, and chose my academics over athletics. I worked the show, received my course credit, showcased my clothing line and got kicked off the team all in the same day. This was a hard decision to make. I had always wanted to play college basketball and being on the team as a potential captain was a dream come true. But it all had to be sacrificed for my academics and debt-free college goal. It was an undesirable sacrifice to make but one that I am happy I made.*

*As a result of not being on the team, for the remainder of my junior year, I focused heavily on my clothing line and academics and returned to the team the following year after a poor season and negotiations with the coach.*

- *During my fourth year of college, there was a time when my money was low. I did not have enough money to eat. Instead of making my friends, mentors, or family members aware, I kept quiet about my situation because I wanted to figure it out for myself. One day when I was walking on campus down "the strip" (a long walkway where students hang out that divides the entire Clark Atlanta University Campus), someone whom I had seen around campus but who did not attend CAU approached me with a proposition. He told me that because I knew so many students, he could pay me $2,000 a week if I sold drugs for him. I quickly thought to myself, I could really use this kind of money.*

  *As great as the deal sounded, I knew that it could not be that simple, and that I was not going to throw away my future and all of the hard work that people invested in me. I refused to place myself in a position where I might have to return home to Vallejo, California, a statistic or disappointment. So I told him that I wasn't interested and went on about my day. I really could have used that money but it wasn't worth jeopardizing how hard I had worked to get to where I was.*

  *Soon after his proposition, something great happened. A friend reimbursed the money I had lent to him—money that I had forgotten about. So everything worked out for the best. That proposition to deal drugs was truly a test of my character. I sacrificed the fast way of solving my financial problem to be the upstanding student that my mentors, community, and family could be proud of. The rewards are far better than they would have been had I agreed to sell drugs. No one can call me an ex-drug dealer and I take pride in that. My decision to not sell drugs is one that I will never regret.*

- *If your funds ever become so low that you can't afford meals, let your friends, family, and mentors know. Desperate times call for desperate measures, and you don't want to be in a position where you are so desperate that you are willing to jeopardize your future in order to survive. Many students fall on hard times, but true friends and family will often assist you without judgment if you do not abuse their generosity.*

- *I was in college for five years because I decided to double major and study abroad during the semester that I was due to graduate. As a result, my second major required an additional year. I had already done my semester budgeting (Strategy #10 Be Financially Smart) and course forecasting (Strategy #7 Master Your Schedule) before I decided to pursue additional academic opportunities.*

STRATEGY

# 3

# BUILD RELATIONSHIPS

Building relationships with people is often overlooked, but it can be beneficial when it comes to financing your education. It is also natural and necessary for maintaining emotional stability.

A financial aid officer will make an extra effort to provide aid that is available to people they know. It is your responsibility to develop relationships with key people who know how to access money for tuition and expenses and who have connections that can assist in paying for your higher education.

This is one of the most important strategies in this book. Most of my scholarship money was obtained by building relationships with key people such as department chairs, financial aid officers, professors, and others.

Think about building relationships the same way you'd think about receiving money from your family. Who are your family members most likely to give their money to? You or a stranger? Almost anyone would give money to family members or people they know before offering it to a stranger.

This is the same mentality you must have with your financial aid counselor. They may not be your parent or family member, but you can be sure that they will give the scholarship money that becomes available to their family, close friends, or people they know before they give it to strangers.

It may not sound fair, but this is the way things work. If you just meet with your financial aid counselor when you need something, why should you be treated any differently from other students? People take care of those they know, and your institution's financial aid advisors, people with influence, and scholarship committees are all operated by caring people. Let's be honest, if you're not building relationships what's the difference between you and the other students on campus.

I'm not suggesting that you try to use your financial aid counselor. Rather, you should build a genuine relationship so that your counselor has a personal connection with you. Your relationship with him or her can actually be the difference between having and not having student loan debt.

My "mom" in the financial aid office took great care of me as if I were really her child. I treated her as if she were really my mom. Her treatment led other staff members to treat me with kindness and respect, and as a result, I continued to receive scholarship money. I kept my grades high and participated in many extracurricular activities, which were the ways I showed my appreciation and support for the assistance they provided.

Knowing that I had someone whom I could talk to because of the relationships that I had built on campus made me feel safer and helped me to continue to excel because I knew I had a support group. Being able to discuss and learn about certain aspects of life with friends totally changed my life.

When people help you, show them your appreciation by doing better than you were before. In the case of your debt-free college education, show your appreciation through proper decorum and academic achievement.

There were students with higher GPAs than mine who could have taken my scholarship away from me. But, based on the fact that I was a well-rounded student with a strong relationship with my financial aid counselor, I was repeatedly awarded institutional and outside scholarships.

Building relationships goes beyond your financial aid counselor. Research and observe who else has influence in the areas in which you need assistance. For example, if there is a scholarship available through your academic department, who would be an understanding and supportive advisor? It may be the department chair or a senior professor. If you don't know who has influence, find out and pay attention to the things that are important to them also. It is not always all about you.

**Remember:** It's your job to have the proper relationships with these decision-makers so that they know who you are when the time comes to award students with scholarships. When appropriate, you should also periodically remind these gatekeepers of your financial need, because there are thousands of students in need of money for school, but many of them are not willing to create and nurture genuine relationships.

When you create stable and nurturing relationships you feel safer to be yourself. You feel that you have people who actually care about your well-being. Feelings of comfort and a sense of family when you are away from home can help you to perform better academically and build better relationships.

There is one platinum rule that you will need to follow when building relationships and that rule is: *Be Genuine*! People can sense insincerity. If they sense that you aren't genuine, then you are worse off than you were when they didn't know you.

***Author's Experiences and Opinions:***

*I received an institutional scholarship consecutively for the following reasons:*

- ***MOST IMPORTANTLY:*** *I did my best academically and met scholarship committees and financial aid counselors halfway so they could reason in my favor.*
- *I established a personal relationship with my financial aid counselor.*
- *I made a name and reputation for myself as someone who worked extremely hard to help himself, which made others want to help me.*

***How to Create and Nurture Relationships with Decision-Makers:***

- *Drop in just to say "hello."*
- *Express gratitude and send thank-you cards often.*
- *Offer your assistance whenever you can.*
- *Make sure that you build relationships with gatekeepers such as secretaries, department aids and work-study students. These individuals often control the access you have to people and privileges that others may have difficulty accessing. People help those who help themselves and are kind to them.*
- *Building relationships is a great way to generate funds for college, but it is also vital to your success in life. The friends you make in college may be for life and may also have connections to jobs after you graduate. Continue to build sincere relationships and a positive rapport with them.*
- *Make thank-you cards your standard.*

STRATEGY

# 4

# MEET EVERYONE HALFWAY

Your DEBT-FREE college education will be a result of the effort that you put into obtaining it. So, in order to gain the best opportunities for scholarship funding and access to decision-makers, you must do your part by performing your best overall and meeting everyone (e.g. scholarship committee members, counselors, parents/guardians, peers, etc.) halfway.

Meeting individual's halfway means developing the following essential elements of character and education in order to become a well-rounded person.

**Meet Everyone Halfway Element #1: Reputation**

People will ask others about you when they see you on campus or come across your name on applications and other materials. Most of the time, you will not be aware of their inquiries. For this reason, it is important to have and maintain a positive reputation. Assist administrators or gatekeepers with tasks in order to show them how determined you are to remain positive and take the necessary steps to obtain scholarship funding, recommendation letters, etc., that ultimately lead to a debt-free college education.

A great reputation inspires trust. People select those who they trust because they know the person will represent their cause or organization well. Your letters of recommendation will speak to your character and work ethic but you have to represent yourself beyond paper and sometimes in interviews. The better you represent yourself overall will result in more opportunities coming your way. People will also seek you out and will be more inclined to help if they hear great things about you. Everyone loves being a part of a success story. Meet everyone halfway with your reputation so that it can bring you opportunities that you were not aware of previously.

**Meet Everyone Halfway Element #2: Extra-Curricular Activities**

Extra-curricular activities expand your network, introduce you to new people, and expand the reach of your positive reputation. These activities sharpen your skills, mind, and ability to adapt to different environments and circumstances. People always want to know what you do outside of your personal tasks, and your extra-curricular activities demonstrate that you are dedicated to causes bigger than yourself. This is a topic often inquired about by decision-makers when you are being considered for scholarships, academic or athletic awards, or career and educational opportunities.

Extra-curricular activities also offer you life-changing experiences such as advanced learning, teachable moments, and exposure to new things. Participating in extra-curricular activities and maintaining a positive reputation will show others that you are responsible and have the ability to multi-task.

**Meet Everyone Halfway Element #3: Academics**

Without the grades you won't get paid. If someone likes your reputation and participation in extra-curricular activities, they can only take you so far on your debt-free college journey without your meeting them halfway academically.

In high school I had friends who broke state records in athletics but were not able to attend college on the full ride scholarships (all expense paid college educations) that were waiting for them. They could not obtain their debt-free college educations because they did not have the minimal grades or test scores for admission. They could not meet the college's/university's requirements halfway and as a result, missed out on life-changing opportunities.

During college I also witnessed peers lose scholarships because of their poor academic performances and as a result, they had to take time off from school or transfer to another college. Maintaining competitive grades is a must; you do not want to have all of the tools (athletic ability, extra-curricular activities, and a good reputation) and allow your academics or one missing element of meeting everyone halfway to be the reason why you would not be selected for or move forward with the opportunities presented to you. Advisors, selection committees, and others can pull your transcript without your knowledge and you can lose opportunities without ever being informed because you are not achieving the academic standard.

This strategy also applies to most of the things you will accomplish in life. Your hard work and determination will equip you with important skills so that you are prepared when your network(s) present you with opportunities.

Henry Hartman says, "Success always comes when hard work meets opportunity." To be successful at obtaining a debt-free college education and other opportunities in life, you must do your part and meet everyone halfway.

***<u>Author's Experiences & Opinions:</u>***

- *Meeting others halfway has resulted in many benefits. I will share a few of the experiences that this strategy has allowed me to have.*

  *When I was a troubled boy on the verge of being kicked out of the Continentals of Omega Boys and Girls Club (COBGC), the founder, Mr. Philmore Graham who became my mentor, took the time to challenge me by using academics and rewards as a technique to change my behavior. He was aware of my academic reputation and rewarded me with sports cards, treats, and other items for correctly answering math and critical thinking questions. So naturally, I began to seek him out on a daily basis in order to earn rewards. The catch was that he would only reward me if I were well behaved. This technique made me meet Mr. Graham halfway by improving my behavior and learning more. With my response to his curriculum-based challenges, I was able to stay in the COBGC program, which resulted in building my academic and social foundation.*

  *In high school, when my ninth grade photography teacher, Ms. Wilson stopped me to ask if I was going to college I told her, "No, I don't have any money or family; I may go to a community college or something." She knew about my academic reputation and responded with, "Oh yes you are; you have too much potential to throw away."*

*Ms. Wilson made it her business to make attending college a reality for me. She spent many hours teaching me how to fill out college applications, scholarships, and the FAFSA. Each time that she showed me something new, I would research it and return with questions or have the task completed, thus encouraging her to teach me more.*

*I was willing to help myself and Ms. Wilson was willing to continue helping me. I also had the academics and extra-curricular activities, and was working on my reputation, so Ms. Wilson was not wasting her time by helping me.*

*When I got to college, Ms. Batey, my professor in the Fashion department, helped me to find money for school and went beyond her teaching duties to teach me more than she was required. Because of my work ethic, Ms. Batey stayed after class to teach me and allowed me to meet her at her weekend sewing classes to learn more. She would often nominate me for opportunities because I possessed all three elements to meet her or any other person to whom she referred me halfway.*

*When it was time for me to move to New York City after graduating college, one of my mentors, Ms. Evelyn "Heart Lady" Polk, financed my living arrangements for my first two months because she trusted me to move to New York, work hard, make a mark, and establish a life here. She knew of my work ethic and expected nothing less. I came to New York and did what she expected—I met her halfway.*

*I have many, many more stories of how meeting others halfway has helped me on my journey. Trust me: I would not be here today or be able to write this book if I did not do my part and present myself as a person who could handle any task put in front of me to the best of my ability.*

*This is a life lesson that is bigger than just a debt-free college education. I strongly encourage you to do your part, come correct, and MEET EVERYONE HALFWAY. Keep in mind that it took time to build relationships (Strategy #3) with each of the people whom I previously mentioned I met halfway.*

STRATEGY

# 5

# APPLY FOR SCHOLARSHIPS

Scholarships are free competitive funds. There are two different types of scholarships: renewable and non-renewable. A renewable scholarship can last more than one semester or academic year. A non-renewable scholarship only lasts for the current semester or academic year. Winning a renewable scholarship is a bonus because you have a higher chance of winning it again due to scholarship committees being familiar with whom you are and your familiarity with their specific scholarship process. Be sure to apply for both types of scholarships with the same effort.

There are thousands of scholarships to apply for and millions of available dollars. Scholarships are free to research, so you shouldn't pay anyone to find scholarships for you. Instead, you should meet with your high school guidance counselor or college academic advisor to discuss what scholarship deadlines, if any, are approaching or are ongoing. You can also research online, with your local organizations or library for various scholarships that best fit you and your goals. To get you started, here are six popular scholarship websites and one app:

- **www.collegeboard.org**
- **www.collegenet.com**
- **www.college.niche.com**
- **www.fastweb.com**
- **www.myscholly.com (app)**
- **www.scholarships.com**
- **www.uncf.org**

The key to winning scholarships is to apply to more than one. It is a numbers game. Applying to one $60,000 scholarship is great, but think about how many other students are applying for the same scholarship. Do not underestimate smaller scholarship awards of $500 or $1,000, because they add up and may be less competitive than larger scholarships.

Another way to think about smaller scholarship amounts is to consider the fact that winning ten different scholarships worth $200 each is the same as winning one $2,000 scholarship.

Apply for as many scholarships as you can. You can also increase your chances of winning free money by applying for scholarships that are unique to you or your background, such as your race, family history, life experiences, hobbies, etc.

For some renewable and non-renewable scholarships, you can use the same information or documentation, but you may need to tweak your application to fit the requirements of each scholarship. To keep a renewable scholarship, you should maintain or increase your level of academic and extra-curricular performance. Most scholarships usually have similar core requirements such as a minimum grade point average (GPA), an essay, letters of recommendation, transcripts, and records of community service and social/extra-curricular activities.

Also, continue to look for scholarships after you are enrolled in college. Ask your friends which scholarships they are applying for in order to maximize your chances. After all, you can never have enough free money.

Some scholarships organizations can run out of funding. Should you lose a $3,000 scholarship due to economic hardships on behalf of the sponsor, and you need $3,000 to enroll loan-free for the current semester, having another $3,000 scholarship available because you made the effort to apply for various scholarships from different sponsors, will help you stay debt-free, and will motivate you to continue applying for scholarships!

Often, institutional scholarships that you were not eligible for when you entered college may become available once you show that you are performing at a higher academic level, or because of your participation in extra-curricular activities. Apply for institutional scholarships every semester, every quarter or at every opportunity.

When you are awarded a scholarship, always send a thank you letter to your scholarship sponsor. If more than one person has helped you with your scholarship process, send out multiple thank you letters. Gratitude is always appreciated and remembered. Thank you letters can help move you to the top of the list for the next award term, or win you recognition with a scholarship committee.

**Applying for scholarships While Meeting Everyone Halfway**

Most people will not be great at all three of the meet everyone halfway elements (reputation, extra-curricular activities and academics). This is where you can become a competitor and steal the show and free money.

You want anyone who inquires about you regarding these three elements to be able to check you off as a great candidate and grant you quick access to proceed further with the opportunity. The easier it is for selection committees, academic and financial aid advisors, or anyone else to check your name off as a great candidate they can trust, the more they will throw your name into other opportunities when asked for candidates to nominate. Why? Because you have made it easy for them by meeting them halfway.

The three elements of meeting everyone halfway that are mentioned in the previous strategy will assist you tremendously in your goal of achieving a debt-free college education. To fully grasp how the Meet Everyone Halfway strategy applies to obtaining scholarships, compare it to persuading your parents/guardian to let you go to a party.

When you want to attend a party you will:

1. Find out exactly who is having the party
2. Obtain the party's location and directions so that you don't get lost
3. Figure out what it will take for your parents to say yes

Once you know all of this information, you will do what is necessary to accomplish your goal, which will most likely include:

1. Doing all of your chores
2. Behaving well in school and in public
3. Doing extra housework

By meeting your parents halfway, it will be hard for them to tell you no. Ironically, this strategy will also assist you in obtaining college scholarships. To see a side by side comparison, review the how to get to a party and how to get a scholarship example on the next page. This tip is also available for download when you sign up for your free $1 million dollar scholarship list on our website **www.debtfreecollegeacademy.com/free**

**HOW TO GET TO A PARTY**

1. Find out who's, when, where, what type of party it is (do you have to bring a gift)
2. Find out what it will take for your parents to tell you yes.
3. Meet Everyone Halfway: Do your chores, behave in school, at home and in public. Complete all homework/ class work and turn it in on time.
4. Wait for a decision from your parents/ guardian (putting the ball in their court and presenting yourself as the most deserving daughter/son to attend the party.)
5. Assist where you can to make sure you arrive on time. (Find the directions to the party instead of waiting for your parents/guardian to figure them out.)

**HOW TO GET A SCHOLARSHIP(S)**

1. Find out who's, when, where, what type of scholarship it is.
2. Find out what it will take for the scholarship committee to tell you yes you've been awarded the scholarship (requirements)
3. Meet Everyone Halfway: Complete the scholarship application, retrieve your transcripts, letters of recommendation, essay etc. Turn in the application on time
4. Wait for a decision from the scholarship committee (putting the ball in their court and presenting yourself and your application as the best candidate for the scholarship)
5. Assist where you can to make sure your application is submitted on time. Create drafts of recommendation letters, take parts of the application to be signed off on or completed by others etc.

In meeting everyone halfway, you may have to go further in order to meet your goal. You may have to assist the scholarship committee; teacher/professors who are writing your letters of recommendation who are busy while you are working on a deadline. Your deadline is most important to you because you need the recommendations. Always make tasks for others as easy as possible. This also shows initiative.

To obtain your debt-free college education, you must find the resources nearest and available to you. Next, you must do the work in order to prepare to use the resource(s). This means that you must do all that you can on your part in order to present yourself and your scholarship application professionally to the person/committee in charge.

**Additional tips to meet everyone halfway for scholarships:**

- Take the initiative to make the connections with people with influence; set appointments, have lunch, have conversations with them to let them know who you are.
- Get your grades to a level where they can compete with other students for free money, join groups and organizations.
- Always finish applications or respond to opportunities as quickly as possible, before deadlines.
- Always have your letters, essays or any work proofread before submitting. (Use the English writing labs on campus, which are usually free)
- Always present your materials and yourself professionally and thoroughly
- Always go back and ask questions if you have them
- Always look to grow and become better, people help those who are helping themselves
- Always show up with knowledge of anything that you are applying for or involved in. This means doing research, prior to the event or meeting.

- Your reputation and peer group all have an impact on how you are perceived on campus. You basically want administrators and peers to know that you are a good person, that you handle business in and out of the classroom and that you should be the first to be recommended for any opportunity. With a good image, you will not have to ask for help as often because people will be looking to help you. It's not always who you know but who knows or knows about you. People observe your attitude and behavior; so be your best at all times.
- If a scholarship requires a 3.0 GPA and there are thirty applicants all with a 3.0 GPA or higher, then the scholarship committee will select the recipient(s) based on other criteria specified in the application. Additional information such as your scholarship essay, community service, leadership clubs, and extra-curricular activities make you a stronger candidate for any scholarship you apply for. Your GPA gets your foot in the door and your extra-curricular activities and overall profile keep the door open. Don't be left outside because your grades can't get you in.

***Author's Experiences and Opinions:***

- *When seeking scholarship money to finance my debt-free college education, I did the following:*

*1) Met individuals halfway by:*

*a) Having a great reputation*
*b) Being involved in volunteer and extra-curricular activities*
*c) Earning competitive grades*

*2) Identified who was in charge of free money for school (sought information from the financial aid office, department offices, professors, online research, etc.).*
*3) Found scholarships for which I was eligible.*

4) *Researched the requirements to obtain the award.*
5) *Knew the key person in charge of the scholarship. After securing an introduction, I established a relationship with that person and inquired about the scholarship.*
6) *Collected the required materials (essay, letter(s) of recommendation, transcript, etc.,)*
7) *Had my materials proofread well before the deadline.*
8) *Requested that the key contact review the application. (The application was already read by an excellent proofreader.)*

   *The reason why I would ask the scholarship key contact person to review my application is so that he or she feels that they have input, which will make them care about it more. It also demonstrates the high level of effort that I am capable of doing early in the scholarship process.*

9) *Made my final application adjustments.*
10) *Submitted the application before the deadline and all the scholarship committee had to do was say yes or no because I completed and submitted a thorough and professional application.*
11) *Followed up with thank you cards to anyone involved in my scholarship process and checked on the award decision periodically.*
12) *Repeated this strategy continuously.*

Download the Debt-Free College Academy Scholarship checklist when you sign up for your free $1 million dollar scholarship list on our website **www.debtfreecollegeacademy.com/free**

**Here are some additional things that I would do to meet everyone halfway for scholarships:**

- *I would always ask for letters of recommendation or any application materials I needed from someone early.*
- *I would always ask for general letters of recommendation so I could use them for multiple purposes.*

- *I would always ask my recommenders if they needed me to write a draft letter that they could easily modify or if they would like a list of the content/ my accomplishments that needed to be expressed in the letter. This saved my recommenders time, helped me meet my deadline and helped me get a letter that says exactly what I needed it to. This is a three in one deal.*
- *I would always make tasks as easy for the other party as possible. For example, if one of my recommenders, advisors or anyone involved in my scholarship application process would say they needed to take something over to be signed by another person whether it was for me or not, I would volunteer to go and do it. This way they did not have to waste their important time doing something so small just for me and so that I could get what was important to me done faster.*
- *I would ask any questions that I had even if I had to keep coming back every day. This showed them that I seriously wanted scholarship money and was willing to work for it.*
- *After a while, people started to send me opportunities because they knew I was qualified (the three meet everyone halfway elements) and how hard I was willing to work/working to find money for school (my reputation).*
- *My grades were much higher in college than they were in high school because I was more serious about my academic performance. I applied and won an institutional scholarship after I was in college and continued to receive the same award every year until I graduated. I didn't have this same scholarship when I first enrolled at my university but my thank-you letters and (strategy #4 meeting everyone halfway) helped me to keep it.*

STRATEGY

# 6

# SUBMIT YOUR FAFSA EARLY

When it's time to go to college, in order to be considered for need-based aid such as free federal and state student grants, work-study, and loans, undergraduate and graduate students must submit a Free Application for Federal Student Aid (FAFSA).

Two important factors that determine how much aid you receive are **1)** your expected family contribution (EFC)[8] and **2)** the amount of time it takes you to submit your FAFSA[9]. If you are a dependent student, you will need copies of your parent/guardian's tax return information from the previous year to complete your FAFSA application. If you are an independent student, you will need copies of your personal tax return information from the previous year to complete your FAFSA application.

If you or your parent/guardian has a delay receiving tax return information the information on your/their W2 tax forms can be used as an estimate to complete the FAFSA application and your estimate can be modified when you receive your tax return. Although the most important thing is completing your FAFSA application as soon as possible, filing your taxes is just as important because they are used to determine your EFC.

---

[8] *The Expected Family Contribution (EFC) is a measurement of your family's financial strength and is calculated according to a formula established by law. Your parent or guardian's taxed and untaxed income, assets, and benefits (such as unemployment or Social Security) are all calculated using the formula. Your family's size and the number of family members who will attend college or vocational school during the same year are also considered. You can use the calculator on www.finaid.org to get an estimate of your EFC.*

[9] *For more information about the FAFSA form or process, visit www.fafsa.gov*

To find out if you are a dependent or independent student, visit **www.fafsa.gov**. Be quick and thorough with your FAFSA application; it becomes available January 1st of each year. Starting in the fall of 2017, the FAFSA application will permanently become available earlier in the year allowing students to complete their applications as early as October 1st. You will also be able to complete your FAFSA application using earlier tax information. For example, on the 2017–18 FAFSA, students (and parents) will report their 2015 income information, rather than their 2016 income information.[10]

Here are 3 ways these changes will benefit you:

1. Because the FAFSA will request earlier year's income and tax information, you will already have your taxinformation by the time you fill out your FAFSA, and you won't need to estimate your tax information and then go back into the FAFSA later to update it.
2. Because you'll already have done your taxes by the time you fill out your FAFSA, you may be able to use the IRS Data Retrieval Tool (IRS DRT) to automatically import your tax information into your FAFSA. (Learn about the IRS DRT at StudentAid.gov/irsdrt.)
3. Because the FAFSA is available earlier, you may feel less pressure and have more time to explore and understand your financial aid options and apply for aid before your state's and school's deadlines.

*Source:* ***https://studentaid.ed.gov/sa/sites/default/files/2017-18-fafsa-updates-students-parents.pdf***

The following table will show you a summary of key dates as we transition to using the early FAFSA submission timeframe and earlier tax information.

---

[10] https://studentaid.ed.gov/sa/about/announcements/fafsa-changes

## EARLY FAFSA SUBMISSION TIMEFRAME

| When a Student Is Attending College (School Year) | When a Student Can Submit a FAFSA | Which Year's Income and Tax Information Is Required |
|---|---|---|
| July 1, 2016 – June 30, 2017 | January 1, 2016 – June 30, 2017 | 2015 |
| July 1, 2017 – June 30, 2018 | October 1, 2016 – June 30, 2018 | 2015 |
| July 1, 2018 – June 30, 2019 | October 1, 2017 – June 30, 2019 | 2016 |

*Source: https://studentaid.ed.gov/sa/sites/default/files/2017-18-fafsa-updates-students-parents.pdf*

To find out more information on the changes to the FAFSA download the FAFSA updates document when you sign up for your free $1 million dollar scholarship list on our website **www.debtfreecollegeacademy.com/free**

Think of the FAFSA as a sweepstakes where the prize is free money to fund your education and you and two million other college students across the United States are all eligible to apply. To enter, you will need to be a full-time student above academic probation and prove your financial need. The earlier you submit your FAFSA, the more money there is available for you, and the sooner you will be awarded.

Applying early also allows you to get a head start on finding additional resources for funding your upcoming academic year. The later you apply, the quicker the pool of money disappears. Obtaining money for college is all about planning and being a few steps ahead of everyone else. Another reason to submit your FAFSA early is because work-study jobs go quickly. Some scholarship committees may require that you share the amount of money you receive in your financial aid package so that they can award you according to your financial need. This means that the earlier you submit your FAFSA, the faster you'll have your requirements for certain scholarships.

Once your FAFSA has been processed, you will receive a letter from your college or university's financial aid office. This important document is called your financial aid award letter. You do not have to accept everything that is in it. For example, you do not have to take the loans that may be offered if you do not need or want to do so. **You have the right to appeal your financial aid award letter!** Because it can vary from institution to institution, you'll need to contact your college's financial aid office to find out about the financial aid letter approval and appeals processes.

An example of why you might appeal a financial aid award letter is if you know that you are going to receive a large scholarship that is based on need but your financial aid award letter has a large amount of loans on it. You would appeal your letter to ask your school to reduce the amount of loans on your award letter so that your financial aid profile shows that you need the entire scholarship amount.

Keeping up with financial aid deadlines and requirements can be a challenge when you are dealing with so many other things on your busy schedule. Use the tracking financial aid worksheet to keep track of your financial aid deadlines. It is available for download when you sign up for your free $1 million dollar scholarship list on our website **www.debtfreecollegeacademy.com/free**

## TRACKING FINANCIAL AID WORKSHEET

| FORMS | DUE DATE | REQUIREMENTS | COMPLETION DATE |
|---|---|---|---|
| | | | |
| COLLEGE APPLICATION(S) | | | |
| | | | |
| | | | |
| | | | |
| | | | |
| | | | |
| | | | |
| | | | |
| FASFA | | | |
| | | | |
| | | | |
| CSS/ FINACIAL AID PROFILE | | | |
| | | | |
| | | | |
| TAX FORMS | | | |
| | | | |
| SCHOLARSHIPS | | | |
| | | | |
| | | | |
| | | | |
| | | | |
| | | | |
| | | | |
| | | | |
| | | | |
| OTHER | | | |
| | | | |
| | | | |
| | | | |

***Author's Experiences and Opinions:***

- *As an independent college student, I was proactive in my effort to obtain money for college, never waiting until the last minute to complete my FAFSA application. I always gathered my documents by mid to late January and completed the application far ahead of the deadline. Next, I would call FAFSA (1-800-4-FED-AID) to follow up to make sure that they didn't need any additional information. Finally, I would periodically follow up with my financial aid counselors until I found out what my award was going to be. Today you can chat live with a FAFSA expert while you are completing your application. Take full advantage of this option and let them walk you through any questions that you may have.*

- ***Remember:*** *There are over two million students applying for the same federal college funding as you. Be pro-active instead of reactive; don't wait to start gathering your documents for your FAFSA application. Have this information available so that your only task is to complete the application online as soon as possible.*

**STRATEGY**

# 7

# Master Your Schedule

If you are not in charge of your schedule, no one else will be. From the moment your parents leave you to your first semester, you are solely responsible for what you achieve during college. You have the freedom to set your own schedule, wake up when you want, and pretty much do as you please.

With so much freedom also comes great responsibility. Your social, study, and personal time as well as a debt-free college education are all dependent on your mastering your schedule. Managing your courses, time, and academic performance will determine your graduation date and how much money you will pay to attend you college or university. Time management and pro-activeness during your matriculation are also essential to your debt-free college experience. This strategy is the key to you getting ahead and remaining on track to graduate on time.

During orientation, most colleges/universities provide every new student with a detailed guide that outlines every major by name, class level, number, and sometimes course description. These are the courses each student enrolling in their respective year is required to take in order to graduate with a degree in the major of study he or she selects. The name of this book may vary from institution to institution, but at my alma mater, Clark Atlanta University, it is called the Course Catalog.

When you receive your course catalog be sure to keep it in a safe place because it will be your guiding light throughout your degree program. If your institution does not provide you with a course catalog, your major's department should have a copy of the set curriculum needed to graduate in your chosen field according to the year you enrolled.

You can also check for a downloadable version of your course catalog on your college's website. There may be multiple catalogs available from previous years because course catalogs are usually updated every few years. It is very important that you keep a copy of the catalog that pertains to your matriculation year.

Your course catalog is very beneficial in the event that you want to change majors or have to take a leave of absence from college. It also outlines the criteria for re-admission and the statute of limitations on credits (i.e., how much time a student can take off before they have to re-enroll under the newest curriculum for his or her major). Be careful not to exceed the allotted time. Each college/university has its own policies on attendance; this is why your course catalog and being informed about your school's policies are very important. You never know what obstacles may arise or who will try to hold you back. If you are aware of the rules, you will be prepared for any challenges that come your way.

For example, at CAU, when a student takes a leave of absence, they must re-apply for admission. Should they wish to take any courses at another college/university, it would be best to check with the registrar (a university's administrative office that is responsible for student records, enrollment procedures, etc.) first to make sure that the courses are transferrable.

At Clark Atlanta University, after six years of time off from initial matriculation, a student seeking re-admission is required to meet any new curricular requirements that may be in effect. After eight years of non-enrollment, a student must re-apply for admission, and must re-take all courses again.

By re-enrolling under a new curriculum, you may need more time to complete your major, and there may be new classes that could require new pre-requisites. This will most likely result in your paying more money to be in school longer. Try to remain in school consistently because requirements to fulfill majors change frequently as a result of evolving technology and new industry methods.

**You are responsible for your graduation!**

This should remain at the front of your mind during your entire time in college. It is your responsibility to remain on track with your courses; you are the only person who can make sure that you graduate on time. Do not rely on your family, friends, or academic advisor. Think of your academic advisor as a consultant who can assist you, but cannot hold your hand throughout your matriculation. Academic advisors have many students. It is important to be pro-active in your effort to graduate because no one else is as invested in your college education as you are.

Mastering your schedule is important. Often, my friends complained about not graduating on time and blamed it on others when it was in fact their responsibility. I have teammates who did not graduate in a timely manner (over 7 years) because they did not master their schedules. They blame everyone else except themselves. Remember you must excel from start to finish.

Graduating on time requires that you know what classes you need to take, what pre-requisites are required, and what semester each class is offered. Check with your major's department, the office of the registrar, or course schedules provided at the end of every semester, for the new and updated class schedules for the next semester.

Pay attention to which classes are usually offered each semester. Knowing this information will help you plan for future class schedules ahead of time. If you have any questions about class availability, be sure to ask the professor(s) who usually teaches the course or the Registrar's office. Each semester equals more money that you must find to obtain a debt-free college education. Make it easy on yourself. Master your schedule!

**Taking classes outside of your major:**

When making your class schedule, always re-check the curriculum guidelines. Try to take required classes that pertain to your major before taking electives (classes that are outside of your major curriculum). If you are a business major with a concentration in marketing, and your dream job is marketing for a television station, take a few classes in the mass communications department. Electives are secondary to completing the curriculum for your major. Even though you have the freedom to pick your classes, you must do so responsibly.

The smartest way to add courses that are outside of your major to your schedule is by using *schedule forecasting*. Set up your class schedule for every semester according to your major requirements. Add in elective classes where you can. Schedule forecasting will help you to prioritize, which classes are most important and which pre-requisites are required so that you do not miss out on the courses you need to graduate.

I forecasted my schedule for my entire matriculation and made adjustments when course availability or times changed. Schedule forecasting provided me with a blueprint that helped me graduate on time. In the event that your schedule does not permit you to take specific courses outside of your major, you can always fulfill an internship within a field outside of your major.

**Figure 3** is an example of what a Fashion Design major's completed *Schedule Forecasting* worksheet looks like. To stay on track to graduate, download this worksheet when you sign up for your free $1 million dollar scholarship list on our website **www.debtfreecollegeacademy.com/free**

## SCHEDULE FORECASTING WORKSHEET

| **FIRST YEAR** | **CREDIT HRS** | | **CREDIT HRS** |
|---|---|---|---|
| **Fall Semester: 16 hours** | | **Spring Semester: 16 hours** | |
| CART 101 Art Foundation I | 3 | CART 102 Art Foundation II | 3 |
| CBIO 101 Biological Science | 3 | CPHY-C 102 Physical Science | 3 |
| CENG 105 English Composition | 3 | CENG 106 English Composition II | 3 |
| CMAT 103 Algebra I | 3 | CMAT 104 Algebra II | 3 |
| CGED 100 First Year Seminar I | 1 | CGED 101 First Year Seminar II | 1 |
| CSOC Social Science Req. | 3 | CCIS 101 Info Tech & Comp. Appl. | 3 |
| **Total Credit Hours** | **16** | **Total Credit Hours** | **16** |
| | | | |
| **SECOND YEAR** | | | |
| **Fall Semester: 15 hours** | | **Spring Semester: 16 hours** | |
| ART 201 Drawing I | 3 | CFAS 237 Fashion Illustration | 3 |
| CFAS 210 Principles of Fashion Industry | 3 | CFAS 230 Textiles | 3 |
| CENG 201/202 World Literature | 3 | CFAS 340 Apparel Construction II | 3 |
| CFAS 240 Apparel Construction I | 3 | HIS-C 202 U.S. Africa&World | 3 |
| CHIS 201 U.S. Africa&World | 3 | CFAS 250 Visual Merchandising | 3 |
| | | CPED 101/2 Phys. Ed. Req. | 1 |
| **Total Credit Hours** | **15** | **Total Credit Hours** | **16** |
| | | | |
| **THIRD YEAR (Study Abroad Option*)** | | | |
| **Fall Semester: Study Abroad (15 hours)** | | **Spring Semester: 15 hours** | |
| CHUM 228 Early Period | 3 | CFAS 320 Draping | 3 |
| CART 277 Computer Imaging Basics | 3 | STA-C 101 Fundamentals of Speech | 3 |
| CFAS 220 History of Costume | 3 | CFAS 360 Fashion Apparel CAD** | 3 |
| CFAS 310 Flat Pattern | 3 | Foreign Language Req. II | 3 |
| Foreign Language Requirement. I | 3 | CPSY 211 General Psychology | 3 |
| **Total Credit Hours** | **15** | **Total Credit Hours** | **15** |
| | | | |
| **FOURTH YEAR** | | | |
| **Fall Semester: 15 hours** | | **Spring Semester: 15 hours** | |
| CFAS 440 Retail Management | 3 | CFAS 420 Fashion Show Production | 3 |
| CFAS 350 Fashion Accessory Design | 3 | CFAS 480 Internship | 3 |
| Fashion Elective | 3 | CFAS 410 Fashion Design Senior Col. | 3 |
| CPHI/CREL Philosophy/Religion Req. | 3 | CFAS 450 Fashion Design Portfolio | 3 |
| Open Elective | 3 | Open Elective | 3 |
| **Total Credit Hours** | **15** | **Total Credit Hours** | **15** |

***Figure 3 Schedule Forecasting worksheet***

**Time and Schedule Management:**

Mastering your schedule goes beyond taking the correct courses in the correct order. It also helps with time management. Creating a master schedule that will help you get ahead during the semester will make your student life much easier and more enjoyable.

Most professors will provide you with a syllabus, an outline of the course and schedule of all work due for his or her class. If you bring all of your syllabi together to plan out which assignments are due first, and complete the small assignments while chipping away at the bigger projects early, it will save you time and headaches. Completing assignments in sections before their deadlines is a lot easier than procrastinating or cramming a day or two before they are due.

The two strategies that we will be using to fill in the master schedule are *assignment scheduling* and *study blocks*. To create an assignment schedule, you must organize the assignments on your syllabi by due dates and study time needed to complete each assignment. If you are uncertain, ask your professor how much time that they think a student should spend in order to complete and submit a completed assignment. For your peace of mind, always try to overestimate the amount of time an assignment will take to complete.

Study blocks are set amounts of time to focus your undivided attention on one subject matter (e.g. English, math, science, etc.). When using study blocks, and in order to use your time most effectively, you have to avoid distractions such as the internet (unless needed for the assignment), phone, peers, music, etc.

Studying in blocks of time with assignment scheduling will allow you to manage and execute the amount of time it will take you to complete a project. For example, if you have an assignment that is going to take five hours to complete and you have a week to finish it, you would mark the assignment's due date on your master schedule and then block out the amount of time per day that you are going to spend completing it. So a five-hour assignment that is due in a week can be broken down into the following different study blocks:

1) Five hours in one day
2) Two and a half hours for two days
3) One hour each day for five days
4) Forty-five minutes for six days

Staying on track with study blocks can also help you to visualize how much social and personal time you have. In college, classes have credit hours which are also called units and at most universities, the maximum credit hours a student can take per semester is eighteen. In some cases, more credit hours can be taken with special permission.

What follows is an example of how an assignment schedule would look for one month. (You will have to do this for every month of the semester.) For this example, we will imagine that a student has received all of his or her syllabi for their classes during the fall semester, and after organizing them, they wrote down or typed out their assignment schedule like the example on the next page.

**Assignment Schedule**

*MWF = Monday, Wednesday, Friday *T,TH = Tuesday, Thursday

| CLASS | TIME | DAY | ASSIGNMENTS DUE | EST. STUDY TIME NEEDED | DATES DUE |
|---|---|---|---|---|---|
| Psychology 101 | 8-9AM | MWF | 1 exam,1 quiz | 9 HRS TTL: 7,2 HRS | 10/2, 10/29 |
| History 201 | 12:05PM-1:40PM | MWF | 1 paper, 1 exam, 1 quiz | 15 HRS TTL: 5,8,2 | 10/17, 10/24, 10/30, |
| English 102 | 10AM -12PM | T,TH | (2) 10-page papers | 5 HRS/ EACH | 10/8, 10/25 |
| Art History 100 | 1PM-2:30PM | T,TH | 1 major project | 20 HRS | 10/31, |

After organizing their assignment schedule, the student should mark the assignment due dates on the master schedule. Their next step would be to plan their study blocks according to the estimated required study time to complete their assignments before they are due. The master schedule would look something like the example on the following page.

## Master Schedule

| Sunday | Monday | Tuesday | Wednesday | Thursday | Friday | Saturday | HRS SPENT STDYG |
|---|---|---|---|---|---|---|---|
| | 1 | 2 | 3 | 4 | 5 | 6 | 12 HRS 45 MINS |
| | Psych. 101 = 8-9am<br>Hist. 201 12-140pm<br><br>30 MINS ENG. PAPER<br>1 HR PSYCH . EXAM<br>45 MINS ART HIST. PROJ | Eng 102=10-12pm<br>Art Hist. 100 = 1-230pm<br><br>1.5 HR ENG. PAPER<br>1 HR PSYCH. EXAM | Psych. 101 = 8-9am<br>Hist. 201 12-140pm<br><br>30 MINS ENG. PAPER<br>1 HR. HIST. PAPER | Eng 102=10-12pm<br>Art Hist. 100 = 1-230pm<br><br>1.5 HRS ENG. PAPER<br>1 HR PSYCH. EXAM | Psych. 101 = 8-9am<br>Hist. 201 12-140pm<br><br>2 HRS ART HIST. PROJ | 2 HRS ART HIST. PROJ | |
| | | | | | | | |
| 7 | 8 | 9 | 10 | 11 | 12 | 13 | HRS SPENT STDYG |
| 1 HR ENG. PAPER<br>1 HR PSYCH. EXAM | Psych. 101 = 8-9am<br>Hist. 201 12-140pm<br><br>1 HR PSYCH . EXAM<br>2 HRS HIST.PAPER<br>45 MINS ART HIST. PROJ | Eng 102=10-12pm<br>Art Hist. 100 = 1-230pm<br><br>1 HR PSYCH . EXAM<br>3 HRS ART HIST. PROJ | Psych. 101 = 8-9am<br>Hist. 201 12-140pm<br><br>1 HR PSYCH . EXAM<br>2 HRS HIST.PAPER<br>1 HR ENG. PAPER | Eng 102=10-12pm<br>Art Hist. 100 = 1-230pm<br><br>1 HR HIST. EXAM<br>1 HR ENG. PAPER | Psych. 101 = 8-9am<br>Hist. 201 12-140pm | 1 HR HIST. EXAM | 16 HRS 45 MINS |
| | 10 PG ENG. PAPER DUE/<br>5 HRS STUDY TIME | | | | PSYCH EXAM/ 7 HRS<br>STUDY TIME | | |
| 14 | 15 | 16 | 17 | 18 | 19 | 20 | HRS SPENT STDYG |
| 2 HRS HIST. EXAM<br>1 HR ENG. PAPER<br>2 HRS ART HIST. PROJ | Psych. 101 = 8-9am<br>Hist. 201 12-140pm<br><br>1 HR HIST. EXAM<br>2 HRS ART HIST. PROJ | Eng 102=10-12pm<br>Art Hist. 100 = 1-230pm | Psych. 101 = 8-9am<br>Hist. 201 12-140pm<br><br>1 HR ART HIST. PROJ | Eng 102=10-12pm<br>Art Hist. 100 = 1-230pm<br><br>1 HR HIST. EXAM<br>45 MINS ART HIST. PROJ | Psych. 101 = 8-9am<br>Hist. 201 12-140pm | | 10 HRS 45 MINS |
| | | | 5 PG HIST. PAPER DUE/<br>5 HRS STUDY TIME | | | | |
| 21 | 22 | 23 | 24 | 25 | 26 | 27 | HRS SPENT STDYG |
| 2 HR HIST.EXAM<br>3 HRS ART HIST. PROJ | Psych. 101 = 8-9am<br>Hist. 201 12-140pm<br><br>1 HR HIST. EXAM<br>45 MINS ART HIST. PROJ | Eng 102=10-12pm<br>Art Hist. 100 = 1-230pm<br><br>1 HR PSYCH. QUIZ<br>1 HR ART HIST. PROJ | Psych. 101 = 8-9am<br>Hist. 201 12-140pm<br><br>1 HR PSYCH. QUIZ | Eng 102=10-12pm<br>Art Hist. 100 = 1-230pm<br><br>1 HR HIST.QUIZ | Psych. 101 = 8-9am<br>Hist. 201 12-140pm | | 10 HRS 45 MINS |
| | | | HIST. EXAM/ 8 HRS<br>STUDY TIME | 10 PG ENG. PAPER DUE/<br>5 HRS STUDY TIME | | | |
| 28 | 29 | 30 | 31 | | | | HRS SPENT STDYG |
| 1 HR HIST. QUIZ | Psych. 101 = 8-9am<br>Hist. 201 12-140pm<br><br>1 HR ART HIST. PROJ | Eng 102=10-12pm<br>Art Hist. 100 = 1-230pm | Psych. 101 = 8-9am<br>Hist. 201 12-140pm | | | | 2 HRS SO FAR |
| | PSYCH. QUIZ/ 2 HRS<br>STUDY TIME | HIST. QUIZ/ 2 HRS<br>STUDY TIME | ART HIST. PROJ. DUE/<br>20 HRS STUDY TIME | | | | |

To complete all of your assignments on time, and stay ahead during the semester, download the Master Schedule template when you sign up for your free one million dollar scholarship list on our website **www.debtfreecollegeacademy.com/free**

Your schedule may or may not be as intense as this example. This is a suggestive template, because this calendar only highlights major assignments and is based upon each student keeping up with class reading, group meetings, etc., which are things that you can just add to the calendar. You will have other responsibilities like work, social and/or organizational commitments etc., but sticking to an assignment schedule will help you master your overall schedule. You can see that in using this calendar, there is still a lot of time left in the week to have fun and hang out. Don't forget to add in time to make connections with people who can get you money for school, research and apply for scholarships, etc. Did you notice that there wasn't a lot of studying on Fridays and Saturdays?

Day-to-day activities change. Even though you may think that you can plan your schedule, it will make it hard for you to adapt when unexpected events occur. That is why we have only filled in the amount of time you need to study during a day for each assignment. Even in a single day unexpected things can pop up and your schedule may have to change. You can adjust these occurrences by turning a one-hour study block into two thirty-minute intervals to fit your changing schedule. When you get your schedule for work, organizational meetings, etc., you will be able to fill them in because they are subject to change, unlike your class times which are constant.

To actively use this calendar, you may sync it with your electronic calendar. Attach it to an application like Evernote, or Google calendar that can keep your master schedule synced on all of your devices (laptop, phone, desktop), put it on a note card or in your binder. The important thing is to have your master schedule where you can see what you must do each day in order to stay ahead during the semester. There are 168 hours in a week. If you spend eight hours a day sleeping, there are still 112 workable hours left for you to master your schedule.

**Here are a few extra tips to help you master your schedule:**

- The earlier in the day that you take classes, the more time you have for yourself and for studying.
- Build your schedule around classes so that you can avoid missing classes or leaving early.
- If you have to build your schedule around your life outside of school, make sure you take a manageable amount of credit hours. Take courses during the times that you are absolutely certain that you can attend in order to avoid missing classes or having to leave early or arrive late.
- Be careful to take only the number of courses that you can handle. If you take courses that you don't think you can handle, withdraw before the deadline in order not to receive a "W" (Withdrawal) on your transcript. Avoid having "W's" on your transcript.
- Pay attention in class and set GPA goals.
- Don't be afraid to work with your classmates; they may have strategies that can assist you with time management.
- Create your own study rhythm. I created my own by mixing my basketball coach's strategy with one of my mentor's schedule.
- Balance school and personal life. Both are equally important.
- Avoid switching majors too many times. Many graduates work in fields other than the one in which they received their degree.
- Do not procrastinate until the night before an assignment is due. It is best to complete assignments before the due dates rather than being under pressure of cramming or scrambling to get things turned in.
- Finishing projects or papers.

- Early completion allows time for a low-pressure review of notes and test material.
- It is important to find out which classes are offered during each semester and which classes you do not have to take consecutively. Some classes may only be offered one semester each year. However, before you can take that course, you may have to take the prerequisite. A prerequisite is a course that you must complete before enrolling in a more advanced course. If your academic advisor is uncertain when a class is offered, ask the professor who normally teaches the course. Being aware of prerequisites and when classes are offered is essential in mastering your schedule. Each semester must be planned strategically.
- Most colleges do not allow students to take courses in their majors at other institutions. Take as many general education courses away from your home institution to possibly save money.

***Author's Experiences and Opinions:***

- *In order to master my college schedule, I was strategic. My college assigned me sixteen credit hours my first semester and expected me to take twelve credit hours the next. After researching that it took 123 credit hours to graduate with a bachelor's degree, I decided I would just take around the same amount they originally assigned me every semester. I knew that a student only had to take twelve credit hours to be full-time but I'm not one to take the easy way out, so I challenged myself. At the end of my first semester, I noticed that there were long lines to get registered for classes and to meet with academic advisors to figure out what classes a student needed to take.*

  *To avoid these lines in the future, I had to be resourceful, so I figured out that my course catalog listed all of the courses I need to take in order to graduate, and I wrote them down by class level and in which semester that I would take them. When the registration period ended, I consulted with my academic advisor and we forecasted my schedule for the duration of my matriculation (Strategy #3 Building Relationships). As a result I knew what courses I would take each year. All that I had to do was pick class times that were available. There were some semesters that I would have to adjust because class times or course availability changed. But for the most part, the same classes were taught during the same semester each year.*

*Schedule forecasting and taking more than twelve credit hours per semester helped me to get an entire semester ahead of my graduating class. Being a semester ahead helped immensely when I decided to work toward a second degree during my fourth year.*

- *The number of credit hours that it takes to obtain a degree varies by major and institution. For my Bachelor's degrees I had to have over 123 hours because I earned two degrees. I actually ended up graduating with 178 hours. But for a student who needs only 123 credit hours to graduate, taking fifteen credit hours per semester for eight semesters (four years) will grant them 120 credit hours. Which means that they will be short on credits and can't graduate in four years. A student would have to take more than fifteen credit hours during one semester or take a summer or winter course. Make sure that you do your schedule forecasting so that you can graduate on time.*

- *When it came to studying for classes I would take all of my syllabi from each professor and put them together to create an assignment schedule. Then I would either estimate out how long it would take me to complete an assignment or ask my professor how long they thought it would take a student to finish and submit a quality assignment. Then I would write it down on my master schedule how much work each assignment required and work on each assignment according to my calendar. This proved to be easier and less stressful than cramming days before assignments were due. My assignment schedule and master schedule also allowed me to plan my evening and weekends. I worked hard to make sure not to have afternoon classes so that I could study early and hang out later. I didn't figure these two strategies out until after I was in college a few years. Schedule forecasting was helpful for me because it allowed me to have flexibility by knowing how many hours I needed to spend on a subject per day.*

- *Two study and social balance strategies that I learned along my journey were to study five days per week and make sure to finish my classes early in the day. My high school basketball coach told our entire basketball team after practice that he only studied from Sunday through Thursday during college so that he could hang out on Fridays and Saturdays. After hearing his story, I decided that I would follow this strategy.*

  *In theory, not studying on Friday and Saturday nights seemed perfect, but when I actually got to college I found out that there were some Fridays and Saturdays that I had to buckle down and study to either get ahead or continue maintaining my grade point average. I had learned to finish my classes early in the day from one of my mentors at the Continentals of Omega Boys & Girls Club. For the most part, I was able to finish my courses early every semester, but there were some semesters when certain classes were only offered later in the evening, and I had to take them.*

- *My study rhythm kept me ahead and when I had to, I studied at night. Everyone's rhythm will be different because everyone has different responsibilities in college that include work, athletics, volunteering, campus organizational commitments, etc. I encourage you to use the tools in this chapter to create your own study rhythm.*

  *Hanging out, partying, emergencies, and responsibility are all going to happen, but when I handled my academics before anything extra-curricular, the consequences were minimal and I didn't have to subconsciously say to myself, "I should be at home or in the library working on an assignment right now." A clear conscience goes hand-in-hand with enjoying oneself.*

- *You can get ahead of your graduating class by taking fifteen or more credit hours over multiple semesters.*

- *When I was considering earning a second degree, I went to the academic advisor in the school of business to discuss the necessary requirements to complete both degrees. By the time I enrolled, the math requirements to receive a degree from the school of business had changed. The academic advisor told me that I must take the new math class. When I returned for our second conversation, I had my course catalog, which stated that any degree I obtained was to be awarded under the established curriculum at the time I enrolled my freshman year. This meant that I did not have to take the new math class because it was not a part of the curriculum when I enrolled at CAU as a freshman.*

  *With that issue out of the way, I also noticed that my second major required a certain number of elective courses to be completed. I asked her if the electives and some of the classes that I had taken as a result of my first degree could be used, which proved to be better than my taking elective courses again. Permission for my former electives and some classes in my first major of Fashion Design/Merchandising was granted and circumstances worked out where I would only have to spend one extra year in school. I knew the statute of limitations on my school's curriculum (using my course catalog) and had planned out how I could obtain my second degree without re-taking courses before signing up. I left the meeting with the academic advisor with the results that I desired.*

STRATEGY

# 8

# THE TWO-FOR-TWO STRATEGY

Not everyone who attends a four-year college or university starts out there. If you have not excelled at the high school level (Strategy 1), or cannot decide which college/university you would like to attend, you should consider attending a community college to complete your general education requirements. The good thing about attending a community college is that they are cheaper than four-year colleges or universities.

While it's sometimes the road less traveled by college students, there are advantages to attending a community college:

- It is affordable; costing just a fraction of the price you would pay to attend a four-year college or university *(See Tables 2 and 3 at the end of this strategy).*
- Financial aid is available to those who qualify.
- You can live at home and work toward an Associate's degree before transferring to a four-year college to earn a Bachelor's degree.
- You will have an opportunity to improve your GPA, which will enhance your chances of getting into the four-year college of your choice.
- You will have enough time to research and apply for scholarships that may cover the cost of your last two years at the four-year college or university of your choice.

Community college is usually affordable to the extent that you can pay for your class expenses out of pocket. Financial aid is also available at community colleges. For example, if a student at a four-year college has $5,000 in grant money, he or she may need an additional $20-25,000 to cover school expenses. With that same $5,000 in grants, a student may be able to cover all of his or her school expenses for the year at a community college.

While pursuing the Two-for-Two strategy, you should always be in contact with your academic advisor to ensure that you are taking the correct courses and staying on track toward earning your Associate's degree. Also, confirm with the four-year college you wish to transfer to that **1)** all courses you take while enrolled in community college are transferrable and **2)** you're taking the correct required courses for your area of study.

It is important to know how many credit hours are transferable so that you do not take more classes than necessary. You do not want to take classes for two years and only be able to transfer partial credits to your four-year college/university.

Being certain that your credits are transferable is your responsibility. Get all commitments, permissions, agreements, etc., in writing and keep them in a special file until your graduation. Use your additional two years to accumulate the resources that you will need to cover tuition and expenses at your four-year college or university. The goal is to be debt-free. Attending a community college at a fraction of the cost of a four-year college is a great starting point.

This is one of the best strategies for achieving a debt-free college education. If my sole objective was the cost of my education, I would have considered enrolling for my first two years at a community college.

***Author's Experiences & Opinions***

- *During my sophomore year, as the school year wound down, I decided that I wanted to take a graphics class in the fall to further enhance the clothing line I had founded. I also decided that it would be smart to take one of my core classes (economics) to get ahead since I would be in school during the summer anyway. Summer school courses at Clark Atlanta University were $365 per credit hour and both classes were three credit hours, so that was $1,095 per course ($2,190 total). I knew that I did not want to take out a loan so I had to figure out a cheaper solution. I did some research and found classes for $12 per credit hour $36 per course ($72 total) at two different community colleges at home in California. After finding my classes, I checked to make sure that they were equivalent to those offered at CAU. I went to my academic department and the Registrar's office and obtained approval for my courses at the community college so that the credits I earned would transfer to CAU.*

  *One class was in the morning and the other was at night. For the majority of that summer, I went to class early in the morning, worked in the afternoon, and went back to class at night.*

  *The two colleges are about an hour apart and I worked and lived in a city between both of them, but in order to avoid student loans and take that graphic design class to help my business, I was willing to do anything.*

  *Let's do the math for the difference in course prices:*

  *Clark Atlanta University: $365 X 3 credit hours = $1,095 per course X 2 = $2,190*

  *California Community College: $12 X 3 credit hours = $36 per course X 2 = $72*

  *The difference in price for one course at community college* *versus at CAU was $1,059! I took two courses that summer and saved $2,118. After doing the math, I took as many courses at California community colleges as I could.*

*This table highlights the estimated cost of public college in the U.S.*

**In dollars. Estimated, for the entire academic year ending in year shown. Figures are average charges per full-time equivalent student. Room and board are based on full-time students]*

| | PUBLIC INSTITUTIONS | | | | | | | | | | | |
|---|---|---|---|---|---|---|---|---|---|---|---|---|
| | TUITION & REQUIRED FEES | | | BOARD RATES | | | DORMITORY RATES | | | TOTALS | | |
| ACADEMIC YEAR | 2-YEAR COLLEGES | 4-YEAR UNIVERSITIES | OTHER 4-YEAR SCHOOLS | 2-YEAR COLLEGES | 4-YEAR UNIVERSITIES | OTHER 4-YEAR SCHOOLS | 2-YEAR COLLEGES | 4-YEAR UNIVERSITIES | OTHER 4-YEAR SCHOOLS | 2-YEAR COLLEGES | 4-YEAR UNIVERSITIES | OTHER 4-YEAR SCHOOLS |
| 2015 | $3,058 | $10,870 | $7,981 | $3,445 | $5,377 | $4,788 | $3,807 | $6,117 | $6,104 | $10,310 | $22,364 | $18,873 |
| 2016 | $3,241 | $11,523 | $8,460 | $3,651 | $5,700 | $5,075 | $4,036 | $6,484 | $6,470 | $10,928 | $23,706 | $20,005 |
| 2017 | $3,436 | $12,214 | $8,968 | $3,870 | $6,042 | $5,380 | $4,278 | $6,873 | $6,858 | $11,584 | $25,129 | $21,206 |
| 2018 | $3,642 | $12,947 | $9,506 | $4,103 | $6,404 | $5,703 | $4,534 | $7,285 | $7,270 | $12,279 | $26,636 | $22,478 |
| 2019 | $3,860 | $13,724 | $10,076 | $4,349 | $6,788 | $6,045 | $4,807 | $7,723 | $7,706 | $13,016 | $28,235 | $23,827 |
| 2020 | $4,092 | $14,547 | $10,681 | $4,610 | $7,196 | $6,408 | $5,095 | $8,186 | $8,168 | $13,797 | $29,929 | $25,256 |
| 2021 | $4,338 | $15,420 | $11,322 | $4,887 | $7,628 | $6,792 | $5,401 | $8,677 | $8,658 | $14,625 | $31,725 | $26,771 |
| 2022 | $4,598 | $16,345 | $12,001 | $5,180 | $8,085 | $7,200 | $5,725 | $9,198 | $9,178 | $15,502 | $33,628 | $28,378 |
| 2023 | $4,874 | $17,326 | $12,721 | $5,491 | $8,571 | $7,632 | $6,068 | $9,750 | $9,728 | $16,432 | $35,646 | $30,080 |
| 2024 | $5,166 | $18,365 | $13,485 | $5,820 | $9,085 | $8,090 | $6,432 | $10,335 | $10,312 | $17,418 | $37,785 | $31,885 |
| 2025 | $5,476 | $19,467 | $14,294 | $6,169 | $9,630 | $8,575 | $6,818 | $10,955 | $10,931 | $18,463 | $40,052 | $33,798 |

***Table 2 Cost of Education Chart*** *- (available for download* when you sign up for your free $1 million dollar scholarship list on the book's website **www.debtfreecollegeacademy.com/free***)*

*For public institutions, data is for in-state students. Beginning 1990, rates reflect 20 meals per week, rather than meals served 7 days a week. Source: U.S. National Center for Education Statistics, Digest of Education Statistics, annual.*

*See also* http://www.census.gov/compendia/statab/2012/tables/12s0293.pdf *or <http://www.nces.ed.gov/programs/digest/>.*

**Extended data beyond the year 2010 has been calculated using a 6% annual increase.*

*This table highlights the estimated cost of private college in the U.S*

**In dollars. Estimated, for the entire academic year ending in year shown. Figures are average charges per full-time equivalent student. Room and board are based on full-time students]*

| | PRIVATE INSTITUTIONS | | | | | | | | | | | |
|---|---|---|---|---|---|---|---|---|---|---|---|---|
| | TUITION & REQUIRED FEES | | | BOARD RATES | | | DORMITORY RATES | | | TOTALS | | |
| ACADEMIC YEAR | 2-YEAR COLLEGES | 4-YEAR UNIVERSITIES | OTHER 4-YEAR SCHOOLS | 2-YEAR COLLEGES | 4-YEAR UNIVERSITIES | OTHER 4-YEAR SCHOOLS | 2-YEAR COLLEGES | 4-YEAR UNIVERSITIES | OTHER 4-YEAR SCHOOLS | 2-YEAR COLLEGES | 4-YEAR UNIVERSITIES | OTHER 4-YEAR SCHOOLS |
| 2015 | $19,907 | $44,583 | $28,429 | $5,875 | $6,377 | $5,627 | $6,982 | $8,751 | $6,553 | $32,764 | $59,710 | $40,610 |
| 2016 | $21,102 | $47,258 | $30,135 | $6,227 | $6,759 | $5,965 | $7,400 | $9,276 | $6,946 | $34,730 | $63,293 | $43,046 |
| 2017 | $22,368 | $50,093 | $31,943 | $6,601 | $7,165 | $6,323 | $7,844 | $9,832 | $7,363 | $36,813 | $67,090 | $45,629 |
| 2018 | $23,710 | $53,099 | $33,860 | $6,997 | $7,595 | $6,702 | $8,315 | $10,422 | $7,805 | $39,022 | $71,116 | $48,367 |
| 2019 | $25,133 | $56,285 | $35,891 | $7,417 | $8,050 | $7,104 | $8,814 | $11,048 | $8,273 | $41,364 | $75,383 | $51,269 |
| 2020 | $26,641 | $59,662 | $38,045 | $7,862 | $8,533 | $7,531 | $9,343 | $11,710 | $8,770 | $43,845 | $79,906 | $54,345 |
| 2021 | $28,239 | $63,242 | $40,328 | $8,334 | $9,045 | $7,983 | $9,904 | $12,413 | $9,296 | $46,476 | $84,700 | $57,606 |
| 2022 | $29,934 | $67,036 | $42,747 | $8,834 | $9,588 | $8,462 | $10,498 | $13,157 | $9,854 | $49,264 | $89,782 | $61,062 |
| 2023 | $31,730 | $71,058 | $45,312 | $9,364 | $10,163 | $8,970 | $11,128 | $13,947 | $10,445 | $52,220 | $95,169 | $64,726 |
| 2024 | $33,634 | $75,322 | $48,031 | $9,926 | $10,773 | $9,508 | $11,795 | $14,784 | $11,072 | $55,353 | $100,879 | $68,609 |
| 2025 | $35,652 | $79,841 | $50,913 | $10,521 | $11,419 | $10,078 | $12,503 | $15,671 | $11,736 | $58,675 | $106,932 | $72,726 |

***Table 2 Cost of Education Chart** - (available for download* when you sign up for your free $1 million dollar scholarship list on the book's website **www.debtfreecollegeacademy.com/free***)*

*For public institutions, data is for in-state students. Beginning 1990, rates reflect 20 meals per week, rather than meals served 7 days a week. Source: U.S. National Center for Education Statistics, Digest of Education Statistics, annual.*

*See also* http://www.census.gov/compendia/statab/2012/tables/12s0293.pdf *or <http://www.nces.ed.gov/programs/digest/>.*

**Extended data beyond the year 2010 has been calculated using a 6% annual increase.*

STRATEGY

# 9

# FIND EMPLOYMENT

Many students work while enrolled in college to cover the costs of tuition, books, and any other expenses. When using this strategy, the balance between work, studying, and social time is vital to your college success. Ideally, you will want to be in a position where you are working because you want to, not because you must. It is a great feeling to be able to focus solely on school and enjoy the full college experience. However, achieving the goal of a debt-free college education requires that you must do whatever it takes.

When looking for employment, it is best to begin researching the jobs or work-study programs your campus offers. This strategy will help you to avoid commuting to and from work. The campus' career center and bulletin boards are good sources for job opportunities.

Once you find a job, you don't want to compromise your GPA or class work by working too much. If you do, you can risk losing certain scholarships, eligibility of certain scholarships, or being placed on academic probation. To avoid this, work study programs offer flexible schedules and federal law states that you can work up to twenty hours per week. If you must work, my suggestions are to work nights, after class, or on weekends when classes are not in session.

Another option to think about is working multiple jobs during the summer, winter, and holiday breaks so that you can devote more time to class work during the school year. **Obtaining an off-campus job during the semester should be your last resort!** If you do work off campus you'll be spending valuable money on transportation that you could be putting toward school expenses.

Other on-campus job options include working as a teacher's or librarian's assistant, joining your student government association (SGA), working in the cafeteria, or patrolling the campus grounds or facilities management.

One on-campus job to also consider is becoming a resident assistant (RA). This job often provides room and board (a place to live and a meal plan) in exchange for your supervision of student residents, providing cultural dormitory programs, and monitoring your residence hall.

***Author's Experiences and Opinions:***

- *Some summers I worked and took classes. During other breaks, I worked full time. To avoid having to work during the school year, I saved my summer earnings to use for school expenses. In addition to working, I sold dinners in my neighborhood to raise money. Without those creative strategies and fundraisers, I would now have student loan debt. So be creative when working in the summer. People are more supportive than you think*

- *I had various jobs on campus throughout my college years; some were work-study and some were not. I was always honest with my employers, letting them know that school was my number one priority. As a result in most situations, I was able to negotiate my schedule.*

- *As a work-study student in my freshman year, I watched the front desk and checked students into my freshman dormitory.*

- *I was an RA during my sophomore year and it proved to be a very enlightening experience. I learned a lot from the residents and about myself. I actually learned to dance the salsa as a result of my producing a dance program with my all-male dormitory and an all-female dormitory. As an RA, I received on-campus housing and a meal plan in exchange for my services.*

- *Another year, I worked as a work-study student being an office assistant in the fashion department.*

- *One of my other jobs during my college matriculation was to go into different offices and survey/rate the way that staff treated students and report my findings to the Retention Services office.*

- *Federal law states that twenty hours is the maximum number of hours a work-study student can work per week. This meant that I had to balance work, schoolwork and my social life.*

*Playing basketball as well as being a designer made it difficult at first, but I selected work-study jobs where I was able to do schoolwork while on duty. This worked out well.*

- *Try to find a job where you can complete class assignments while working.*

STRATEGY

# 10

# BE FINANCIALLY SMART

Though college can be the best part of your life, it can also be one of the most difficult financial times of your life. While achieving your debt-free college education, budgeting will be an absolutely necessary skill. **DO NOT, and I repeat, DO NOT TAKE ANY CREDIT CARDS UNLESS YOU ABSOLUTELY MUST.** If managed correctly, credit cards can help establish good credit. However, you must be responsible. Credit cards are not free money and the balance you place on them should be looked at as debt that needs to be paid as soon as possible. Do not obtain credit cards because you want to buy clothes, a car, a vacation, or have some fun. Trust me: building credit in college is not a requirement. Save the luxuries until after you have obtained your debt-free college education.

*Before we go any further in this strategy let's understand the following:*

An ***asset*** is something that makes a profit periodically or when it is sold.

A ***liability*** is something that takes money away from you or loses money when it is sold.

| **ASSETS** | **LIABILITIES** |
|---|---|
| Cash | Mortgage |
| House | Clothing |
| Rental Property | Car |
| Stocks, bonds & mutual funds | Student loans (other loans) |
| Retirement accounts (401(k) and IRAs) | Credit card debt |

Do not spend all your money on liabilities. Use your money wisely. Don't just spend it to be spending. You must budget for your expenses—necessities, fun, and other areas of your life. When budgeting, be as specific as possible. Should you need to increase your income, be creative and save change when you break a dollar, or sell dinners door-to-door like I did. If you need to save money, be disciplined.

Do not purchase a new car, live beyond your means, or obtain a credit card unless you absolutely need one. If you are on a limited budget, you should not be eating out at restaurants every day, buying new clothes, or going on expensive dates. You must be resourceful and find whatever free or inexpensive (cheap) options are available. Remember the people who are signing starving college students up for credit cards in exchange for free gifts are not there to help you. They are there to make money and credit card companies make the most money as a result of missed payments, not to mention the administrative fees after accounts have gone into collections.

In college, you will see that other students receive refund checks from their college loans. Instead of giving the money back to student loan lenders, often they will spend it on liabilities such as cars, clothes, or other purchases that seem good at the moment. Remember that any amount of money borrowed for college must start being repaid six to nine months after graduation. By being financially smart, you may feel like you don't have the same things other students have at times, but believe me, they will wish they had your freedom when their student loans kick in, especially if they have difficulty finding a job after college. If you can master the skill of budgeting to gain a debt-free college education this skill will assist you later on in life. A financially smart mindset is priceless and is very helpful for purchases of all sizes.

By staying debt-free in college, you have a higher chance of having a favorable credit score post-college, which can help you get the best interest rates on purchases that rely on your credit score. However, a debt-free college education does not always equal a favorable credit score. A great credit score depends on handling your payments responsibly. Being financially smart is not only an important lesson in being a debt-free college student; it is also a critical factor in living a debt-free life.

When you sign up for your free $1 million dollar scholarship list on our website **www.debtfreecollegeacademy.com/free**, you will receive access to a free video tutorial that teaches you how to budget for each semester of college. You will also receive a free Microsoft excel semester budgeting spreadsheet download that will calculate all of your college financial information. This spreadsheet will help you see where you are in terms of needing more or less scholarship money.

I used a semester budgeting worksheet every year that I was in college. It assisted me in achieving my debt-free college education. On the following page is an example of the semester budgeting worksheet.

# SEMESTER BUDGETING WORKSHEET

SEMESTER ______________
YEAR ________________

| INCOME | ESTIMATED | ACTUAL |
|---|---|---|
| GRANTS | $ | $ |
| SCHOLARSHIPS | $ | $ |
| JOB (SALARY) | $ | $ |
| PARENTS | $ | $ |
| SAVINGS | $ | $ |
| WORK-STUDY | $ | $ |
| PUBLIC BENEFITS | $ | $ |
| SPOUSE SUPPORT | $ | $ |
| OTHER | $ | $ |
| INCOME TOTALS | $ | $ |
| ACADEMIC EXPENSES | ESTIMATED | ACTUAL |
| TUITION | $ | $ |
| FEES | $ | $ |
| BOOKS | $ | $ |
| SUPPLIES | $ | $ |
| OTHER | $ | $ |
| ACADEMIC EXPENSE TOTALS | $ | $ |
| LIVING EXPENSES | ESTIMATED | ACTUAL |
| ROOM / RENT | $ | $ |
| BOARD/ MEALS | $ | $ |
| UTILITIES (WATER, GAS, ELECTRIC, TRASH & SEWAGE) | $ | $ |
| PHONE | $ | $ |
| TV (CABLE, DVDs, ETC) | $ | $ |
| TOILETRIES | $ | $ |
| LAUNDRY / DRY CLEANING | $ | $ |
| CREDIT CARD PAYMENTS | $ | $ |
| TRANSPORTATION (GAS, PARKING, INSURANCE, ETC) | $ | $ |
| OTHER | $ | $ |
| LIVING EXPENSE TOTALS | $ | $ |
| PERSONAL EXPENSES | ESTIMATED | ACTUAL |
| BARBER/ SALON | $ | $ |
| ENTERTAINMENT (MOVIES, MUSIC, EVENTS, DINING OUT) | $ | $ |
| CLOTHING | $ | $ |
| TRAVEL | $ | $ |
| OTHER | $ | $ |
| PERSONAL EXPENSE TOTALS | $ | $ |

| | | ESTIMATED | ACTUAL |
|---|---|---|---|
| INCOME | A. TOTAL INCOME | $ | $ |
| EXPENSES | TOTAL ACADEMIC EXPENSES (FROM ABOVE) | $ | $ |
| | TOTAL LIVING EXPENSES (FROM ABOVE) | $ | $ |
| | TOTAL PERSONAL EXPENSES (FROM ABOVE) | $ | $ |
| | B. TOTAL EXPENSES | $ | $ |
| START WITH LINE A THEN SUBTRACT LINE B<br>TO GET YOUR NET INCOME<br>(INCOME MINUS EXPENSES EQUALS MONEY FOR SAVINGS) | | $ | $ |

***<u>Author's Experiences and Opinions:</u>***

- *At the end of each semester I estimated my income for the following semester. During my junior year I estimated my income for my senior year. After creating a budget, I thought about and researched where I could save money. I noticed that the cost to stay in on-campus housing was close to $6,000 for nine months. On-campus housing was fun and many of my friends lived in the dorms, but I sought out a less expensive opportunity.*

  *One of my good friends from California lived with students in a boarding house within walking distance of campus for $300 per month, all utilities included ($3,600 a year). When I did the math, I noticed that I could save almost $2,400, avoid taking out a loan for school, and avoid moving/storage expenses at the end of each break in the academic year.*

  *I moved into the boarding house and saved more than just $2,400: because the $2,400 that I would have borrowed to pay for on-campus housing would have had to be repaid with interest. Budgeting for each academic year was a consistent method that I used to save and avoid loans.*

Remember there is no one right way to achieve your debt-free college goal. I used a combination of these strategies and today I enjoy post-college freedom on a totally different level than those who financed college with student loans. Start creating your plan NOW and use the ten strategies and other resources in this book to earn your debt-free college education.

# QUICK TIPS

When applying to college, remember to use these quick tips. They can save you tons of time and money in the future!

- Consider cost as a primary factor.
- Apply to multiple schools and weigh all of the financial aid packages; try to negotiate for a better financial aid package if necessary by telling financial aid officers what other schools are offering you.
- Look at each of your potential schools' graduation rates, and the average length of attendance. Is it 4, 5, or 6 years?
- Consider financial aid safety schools (schools that you can attend and pay for without financial aid).
- Don't go to for-profit colleges. They can shut down by filing bankruptcy and leave you with student loan debt and no degree.

**More tips:**

- Get informed and be proactive about the financial future of college and your life.
- The amount of United States student loan debt is now over 1.3 trillion dollars and rising; don't allow yourself to be included in this total.
- Admissions officers are like sales representatives for their respective colleges. Their job is to attract the biggest student body and get low acceptance rates to boost their college's rankings.
- A financial aid officer's job is to make sure that students pay their tuition and fees. Unless you establish a relationship with some of them, you'll need to be aware of your financial standing as a student. Be focused and know what's going on with your financial aid account at all times.
- Always try to renegotiate your financial aid packages to receive as much free money as possible.
- Ask family and friends to invest in your education.

- All financial aid information that you receive, as well as checks and balance statements, need to be in writing and kept stored in a safe place until after you graduate.
- The option to test out of classes is sometimes offered when you get to college. You should actively look for and try to take advantage of opportunities to test out of classes because it can free up your time to earn money and research scholarships for the current or upcoming academic year.
- Check with your high school counselor and the college/university you would like to attend. Their Continuing Studies or Registrar's office will have more information on the availability of tests.
- Remember to build strong relationships with people who are able to help you continue your education.
- If you receive a large scholarship in your financial award letter, always ask your financial aid advisor to reduce your loans so that you can show a need to receive the entire scholarship. Sometimes scholarship amounts are reduced because a student is offered a lot of money in student loans.
- Actively pursue scholarships, work-study, grants, and other types of financial aid that do not require you to pay the money back.
- Work hard for your debt-free college education by applying for scholarships and grants and you'll reap the rewards later.
- There are over 20.2 million other students applying for the same federal college funding as you. Be pro-active instead of reactive. Don't wait until after January to start gathering your documents for your FAFSA application. Remember starting Fall 2017 the FAFSA application becomes available October 1.
- Don't switch majors or transfer to another four-year college. These changes may invite unforeseen financial issues. Keep in mind that many people have careers outside of their majors.
- Find out which courses can be taken at community colleges. Take those courses during the summer or winter breaks either back home, or near your school. It is a cheaper way to help pay for four years of college.

- If you must work, try to work part-time during the school year and full-time during the summer to earn money for college. Working during these times will allow you to have time to focus on your courses and course work.

Twitter: @KevinYBrown | Facebook.com/KevBrown001

# Congratulations!
# You have completed 10 Ways Anyone Can Graduate College Debt Free 2.0.

I am proud of you and I am excited to read your review of this book. I would love to help you on your journey. You can contact me to ask any questions via social media and send me updates of your debt free college journey. My social media handles are on the footer of the pages of this book and on the book's website.

In appreciation I am offering a discount of 10% on our Debt Free College Academy courses. Use discount code: **DFCA10.** You deserve it and most of all you have earned it. See the Program overview on the following page.

**I wish you success on your Debt Free College Journey and Beyond.**

**Sincerely,**

**Kevin Y. Brown**

| STARTER KIT | CRASH COURSE | FULL COURSE |
|---|---|---|
| $10 Million Dollar Scholarship list | $10 Million Dollar Scholarship list | $10 Million Dollar Scholarship list |
| $10 Million Dollar Scholarship Checklist | $10 Million Dollar Scholarship Checklist | $10 Million Dollar Scholarship Checklist |
| College Finance 101 Video Training | College Finance 101 Video Training | College Finance 101 Video Training |
| Semester Budgeting Video Training | In-depth FAFSA 101 Video Training For Those Starting the Application immediately | In-depth FAFSA 101 Video Training For Those Starting the Application immediately |
| Semester Budgeting Video Training Worksheet | Semester Budgeting Video Training And Worksheet | Early FAFSA Prediction Video Training For Those Starting Early |
| Debt - Free College Blueprint Poster | Debt - Free College Blueprint Poster | Semester Budgeting Video Training And Worksheet |
| 3 Debt Free College Strategies Document | Complete 12 Lesson Debt Free College Course (Audio only) | Live Debt -Free College 101 Presentation To Over 600 University Students (Audio) |
| 1 Year of Technical Support & Core Updates | Complete 12 Lesson Debt Free College Course Presentation Slides To Each Module | Debt - Free College Blueprint Poster |
| | Resource Worksheets for all 12 Sessions | Complete 12 Lesson Debt Free College Course (Video) |
| | 1 Year of Technical Support & Core Updates | Complete 12 Lesson Debt Free College Course Presentation Slides To Each Module |
| | | Resource Worksheets for all 12 Sessions |
| | | Two (2) Bonus Sessions + Presentation Slides & Worksheets to both Modules |
| | | 1 Year of Technical Support & Core Updates |

# 125 DORMITORY ESSENTIALS CHECKLIST*

It is easy to forget the small things when buying for your big move into your college dorm room.

Your school should provide you with a checklist, but often, the list is short and does not include all essential items. Every college is different and your needs, as well as what is acceptable in your dormitory, will vary from institution to institution. Be sure to only bring those things that you will actually use.

If you are attending college out of state, you don't have to take a lot with you because you can buy items when you arrive. It is also a good idea to purchase all necessities before your parent or guardian leaves. After all, it's better to spend their money than yours. To help you remember the essentials, here is a checklist of 125 things that you may need for your dormitory:

* This checklist is available for download when you sign up for your free $1 million dollar scholarship list on our website **www.debtfreecollegeacademy.com/free**

# 125 DORMITORY ESSENTIALS CHECKLIST

**DORM ROOM**
- ❐ BED ACCESSORIES
- ❐ DECORATIONS
- ❐ STORAGE BINS
- ❐ ALARM CLOCK
- ❐ PERSONAL FAN
- ❐ RUG
- ❐ PHONE

**CLOTHING & ACCESSORIES**
- ❐ SHIRTS/TOPS
- ❐ PANTS/SHORTS
- ❐ SWEATSHIRTS
- ❐ FORMAL ATTIRE
- ❐ WORKOUT CLOTHING
- ❐ UNDERWEAR
- ❐ SOCKS
- ❐ SHOES
- ❐ SLIPPERS
- ❐ BELT(S)
- ❐ PAJAMAS
- ❐ ROBE
- ❐ WATCH
- ❐ JEWELRY
- ❐ SHOWER SHOES
- ❐ WINTER GEAR
- ❐ SWIM GEAR
- ❐ RAIN GEAR

**BATHROOM**
- ❐ MOUTHWASH
- ❐ TOOTHBRUSH
- ❐ TOOTHPASTE
- ❐ DENTAL FLOSS
- ❐ RAZORS/SHAVING CREAM
- ❐ SHAMPOO/CONDITIONER
- ❐ SOAP/BODY WASH
- ❐ HAIR DRYER
- ❐ CHAPSTICK
- ❐ TWEEZERS
- ❐ COMB/BRUSH
- ❐ MAKEUP
- ❐ GLASSES /CONTACTS
- ❐ TAMPONS/PADS
- ❐ DEODORANT
- ❐ Q-TIPS
- ❐ NAIL CLIPPERS
- ❐ HAIR STYLING PRODUCTS
- ❐ PERFUME/COLOGNE
- ❐ SKIN MOISTURIZERS
- ❐ WASHCLOTHS & TOWELS
- ❐ PERSCRIPTION MEDICINE
- ❐ SHOWER CADDY

**DESK & ACADEMIC**
- ❐ STICKY NOTES
- ❐ DRY ERASE BOARD
- ❐ DESKTOP ORGANIZERS
- ❐ CALENDAR
- ❐ BACKPACK
- ❐ PENS AND PENCILS
- ❐ NOTEBOOKS/BINDERS
- ❐ LINED/BLANK PAPER
- ❐ PAPERCLIPS
- ❐ HOLE PUNCHER
- ❐ RULER
- ❐ FOLDERS
- ❐ STAPLER/STAPLES
- ❐ HIGHLIGHTERS
- ❐ SCISSORS
- ❐ INDEX CARDS
- ❐ STAMPS/ENVELOPES
- ❐ CALCULATOR
- ❐ TAPE
- ❐ ETHERNET CABLE
- ❐ COMPUTER
- ❐ EXTENSION CORD
- ❐ 2/3 PRONG ADAPTERS
- ❐ LAPTOP CASE/ BAG
- ❐ USB DRIVE
- ❐ PRINTER
- ❐ DESK LAMP
- ❐ CAMERA
- ❐ MP3 PLAYER

**LAUNDRY/LINEN**
- ❐ LAUNDRY DETERGENT
- ❐ BLEACH
- ❐ FABRIC SOFTENER
- ❐ LAUNDRY BAG/SORTER
- ❐ STAIN REMOVER
- ❐ IRON/IRONING BOARD
- ❐ STARCH
- ❐ HANGERS

**CLEANING**
- ❐ BROOM/MOP/VACUUM
- ❐ ALL-PURPOSE CLEANER
- ❐ CLEANING SPONGES
- ❐ FABRIC ODOR REMOVER
- ❐ AIR FRESHENER
- ❐ DISH LIQUID
- ❐ TRASH CAN
- ❐ TRASH BAGS

**SNACKING**
- ❐ MINI-FRIDGE
- ❐ MICROWAVE
- ❐ DISHES/GLASSWARE
- ❐ DISH SOAP
- ❐ SCRUBBING PADS
- ❐ CAN OPENER
- ❐ PAPER TOWELS

**HARDWARE & STORAGE**
- ❐ HOOKS (ALL SIZES)
- ❐ SURGE PROTECTOR
- ❐ EXTENSION CORDS
- ❐ DUCT TAPE
- ❐ SHELVES & BRACKETS
- ❐ BOOKSHELVES
- ❐ CLOSET ORGANIZER
- ❐ SHELF & DRAWER LINERS
- ❐ CURTAINS & HARDWARE
- ❐ LIGHT BULBS
- ❐ TOOLS (HAMMER, SCREWDRIVER, NAILS)

**FIRST AID BOX**
- ❐ BAND-AIDS
- ❐ ANTIBIOTIC OINTMENT
- ❐ TWEEZERS
- ❐ GAUZE / TAPE
- ❐ HYDROGEN PEROXIDE
- ❐ RUBBING ALCOHOL
- ❐ THERMOMETER
- ❐ ACE BANDAGE
- ❐ FREEZABLE ICE PACK

**IMPORTANT DOCUMENTS**
- ❐ DRIVER'S LICENSE
- ❐ SOCIAL SECURITY CARD
- ❐ BIRTH CERTIFICATE
- ❐ PASSPORT
- ❐ HEALTH INSURANCE INFORMATION

# ACKNOWLEDGEMENTS

To Keyana Brown— I became a good person, student, and athlete because of the example and morals you showed me when I was a young boy. I finally got my 4.0 just like you even though it was thirteen years later. Thanks for everything you did for me growing up sis.

To Ms. Mary Elizabeth Jackson—without you, there would be no one to thank for my completion of this project. After spending less than an hour with me in the children's shelter, you took me home with you to Vallejo, California. Because you never gave up on me—no matter how many of your relatives told you to send me back because I was hopeless—I stand today as an example of what unconditional love and hope can do for a person.

I love you, and I thank you from the bottom of my heart. May you rest in peace.

Your Son,

-Kevin.

To my dearest Marie Elizabeth Dutton Brown—your guidance as a mother figure and mentor has been and continues to be a life-changing experience. You have believed in me since we met, and with your grace of the "412 Experience," this project is possible. I cannot describe the difference you have made in my life. To call you an angel is an understatement of what you are to the world and to me. I love you. Thank you for all that you do and most of all, thank you for being you, an *Original* in every sense of the word!

To Mr. Pelton Stewart—you started me off on the path to leadership with Torch Club (known as the Mighty Oaks Torch Club today) at the Continentals of Omega Boys and Girls Club. At the age of seven, you challenged me to keep at least one form of I.D., a watch (because I should always know what time it is), and to have knowledge of my local and federal government.

Torch club was a huge part of my foundation and you were the architect. Thank you for all of your hard work and dedication over the years.

To Mr. Philmore Graham—words cannot express the everlasting impact that you have on my life. At the age of nine, when I was constantly causing trouble and spending lots of time at the Continentals of Omega Boys and Girls Club, you saved my future. I remember the staff members wanting to give up on me but instead of allowing me to be kicked out of the club, you took the situation into your own hands and challenged me, starting with a question that I will never forget: "What weighs more? A pound of bricks or a pound of feathers?" After answering, "A pound of bricks," you explained to me that they both weighed a pound. From that day forward, you had my full attention. From that experience, you groomed me to understand the rewards and importance of education. The impact of "Study Hall," Keystone, Smart Moves training, the continental honor, and our walks on the Vallejo city waterfront all played a huge part in my making a conscious decision to stay on the road less traveled. I appreciate you for how you changed my life, Mr. Graham. Thank you!!!

To Ms. Carrie S. Wilson—you changed the course of my life after one of my high school basketball games when you asked, "Kevin Brown, are you going to college?" Through your tireless efforts and teachings, I achieved a higher education academically and continue to do so in life. Your teachings beyond the classroom have impacted me eternally, and I am forever grateful to have known Mr. Wilson (a terrific father figure), Kimberly, and Geoffrey. The Wilson family has shaped me. Thank you for everything; I love you all!!!

To Ms. Evelyn "Heart Lady" Polk—you are a mother figure and a positive role model in my life. Since meeting you at the Boys and Girls Club when I was in high school, you have encouraged me to maximize my potential. You started me on my way to New York in the summer of 2008 and are truly an angel with a huge heart. Thank you God Mom "E"!!!

To The Gross Family—Thank You for your continued support over the years, you inspired me to want more out of life.

To the Clark Atlanta University (CAU) staff and faculty you changed me from an eighteen-year-old kid fresh off of the plane from California to a well-traveled man of the world. Thank you for introducing me to our mantra "I'll Find A Way Or Make One." which helped me achieve a debt-free college education. Without you all, I truly would not be able to write this project. Thank you for helping me grow as a person. I would like to extend special thanks to Mrs. Dorothy Batey, Mr. Tolbert, Mr. Hickey, Mrs. Ragsdale, Ty from the print shop, Jason Richardson, Mrs. Morgan, Dr. Jenkins, Ms. Beverly Ferguson-Barrett, Dr. Muhammad Bhiuyan, Ms. Jackie Davis, Dr. Paul Brown, Dr. Dennis Kimbro and the rest of the staff that was present during my matriculation at CAU.

To Dr. Raphael Moffett — You are the best big brother a person can ever have. Every since the ice breaker we did my first week of college, to my request of you being my mentor, to waking up every morning at 7am to work out so I could make the basketball team and all of my other endeavors. You have been there every step of the way, for every accomplishment. Moff, your influences made my matriculation through Clark Atlanta a true growing experience and as I grow to know more about life you still impact me. Without you I would not be where I am today in the same style and fashion. Thank you for being a model for what a great man is and what a role model should be.

To Mrs. Dorothy Batey — An angel and mother figure. You stopped me from switching my major from Fashion Design and in return opened up the world of design to me. Your tireless work as a teacher and mentor in the fashion department is why I excelled as a CAU student in domestic and international study environments. Your standards and expertise have lit up the path and I can assure you that I will continue to follow it. Thank you so much for everything Mrs. Batey.

To Mr. Javier Tolbert —Thank you for your attention to detail and the high standard that you held all of your fashion design/merchandising students to. Because of your influence I understand professionalism, spacing and a standard that you would be proud of. I thank you for your influence and level of expectation. I promise to carry on this standard.

To all of my fellow CAU Panthers who continue to achieve—you push me to become better. Thank You!!!

To Mike Stu – Thank you for being a true friend over the years. From Vallejo to Atlanta, through my first clothing company KAY 1 Apparel and even in the present. You have always been a person that I can count on. I love you bro. I look forward to the future as we evolve.

To the Alvarez family—Thank you for introducing me to New York and for your continued family support throughout my journey.

To Lester Edwards—Thank you for your undying support and leadership through tremendous odds during my time working under you. You gave me the opportunity to remain in New York and follow my dreams. You are a great man.

To the Jackson family—Thank you for your continued love and support over the course of my life. The foundation was laid in my early years and you have been with me throughout my journey. - I love you all.

To John C. White—our initial conversation about this project encouraged me to see it through to completion. Thank you for always believing in me. Thank you for being my friend.

To Aleesha Nash (aka A. Nash) "The Legend"—my partner in grind, friend, and bawse, lol. Thank you for believing in this project and me. You have been on board since day one and your tireless efforts and sense of humor are greatly appreciated. Thanks to your irreplaceable talents, this project was taken to unexpected heights and is possible. Thank you for being you and understanding “THE STANDARD” lol.

To my friend and brother Carl Bowen—thank you for your encouragement and support during this project.

To my friend and brother Eric Fondren—thank you for your encouragement and support during this project.

To Victoria Merriweather and Avia Hicks-Chapman—thank you both for your support on this project.

To Nick Ferris—thank you for allowing me to use your article “Ten Ways Anyone Can Go to College With Zero Student Loans” as a source of inspiration for this book. www.punnymoney.org is a great and humorous resource for financial management.

It is impossible to thank everyone who has influenced and offered me messages to share with others. So I apologize to all of my supporters, fans, and friends not listed here. I appreciate you.

To my current and future peers in the higher education realm— work hard to achieve the freedoms you deserve—especially the freedom of a debt-free college education.

To my current and future peers in the expert community—I am honored to be among you. This field is filled with individuals who inspire, and through teaching others, share their knowledge, experiences, and advice. To all: Continue to change lives.

Twitter: @KevinYBrown | Facebook.com/KevBrown001

# ABOUT THE AUTHOR

Kevin Y. Brown is the founder of debtfreecollegeacademy.com and an authority on how to attend and graduate from college debt-free. He also lectures on personal leadership and maximizing potential and resources. He hosts the radio show and podcast the Create Your Life series on New York City's WHCR 90.3 FM. Live Sundays 5:30-6:30 pm, which is also streamed online at fb.com/Kevbrown1

By building and maintaining positive relationships with Clark Atlanta's professors and administrators, and doing all that was necessary to "meet everyone halfway," Kevin strategically made his way through college without student loan debt.

Since graduating, Kevin has been a college expense and tuition consultant helping families identify resources for a debt-free college education.

Meet Kevin online and receive free college financial training at

**www.debtfreecollegeacademy.com**

## SEMINARS BY KEVIN Y. BROWN

Debt – Free College 101

Create Your Life

Molding A Brand

Diversity U

Learn more about Kevin at

**www.kevinybrown.com**

# BIBLIOGRAPHY

"About Us." *Student Aid on the Web*. Federal Student Aid, 30 June 2011. . 21 June. 2016. <http://studentaid.ed.gov/PORTALSWebApp/students/english/aboutus.jsp>.

"Consequences of Student Loan Default." *TG Online*. Texas Guaranteed Student Loan Corporation, 15 Sept. 2011. Web. 21 June. 2016. <http://www.tgslc.org/borrowers/default/consequences.cfm>.

"Federal Student Aid - Title IV Programs." *Federal Student Aid - Information on Grants, Student Loans, Scholarships and Other Financial Aid*. Federal Student Aid, 28 June 2010. Web. 22 Oct. 2011. <http://federalstudentaid.ed.gov/about/title4_programs.html>.

.Kantrowitz, Mark. "FinAid | Loans | Defaulting on Student Loans." *FinAid! Financial Aid, College Scholarships and Student Loans*. Mark Kantrowitz. Web. 21 June. 2016. <http://www.finaid.org/loans/default.phtml>. (student loan default)

Kantrowitz, Mark. "FinAid | Student Loans." *FinAid! Financial Aid, College Scholarships and Student Loans*. Mark Kantrowitz. Web. 21 June. 2016. <http://www.finaid.org/loans/>.

"License Revocations | Student Loan Borrower Assistance." *Student Loan Borrower Assistance | A Resource for Borrowers, Their Families and Advocates*. National Consumer Law Center. Web. 22 Oct. 2011. <http://www.studentloanborrowerassistance.org/collections/government-collection-tools/license-revocations

U.S. Census Bureau 2012. "Table 293 INSTITUTIONS OF HIGHER EDUCATION-AVERAGE CHARGES" *12s0293.pdf*

DiGangi, Christine. "The Class of 2016 Will Graduate With an Average of $37,172 in Debt." *Fox Business* 6. May. 2016. Web. 18 June. 2016. <http://www.foxbusiness.com/features/2016/05/06/class-2016-will-graduate-with-average-37172-in-debt.html>

DiGangi, Christine. "The Class of 2016 Will Graduate With an Average of $37,172 in Debt." *Time* 5. May. 2016. Web. 19 June. 2016. < http://time.com/money/4319569/graduate-student-debt-class-of-2016/>

The Institute for College Access & Success. 2014. Quick Facts about Student Debt. http://bit.ly/1QcRwmn

Bureau of Labor Statistics, "Earnings and unemployment rates by educational attainment Table: ep_table_001" *U.S. Department of Labor* 15. March, 2016 Web. 19 June. 2016. *<http://www.bls.gov/emp/ep_table_001.htm>*

Mitchell, Josh. "More Than 40% of Student Borrowers Aren't Making Payments." *Wallstreet Journal* 7. April. 2016. Web. 19 June. 2016. <http://www.wsj.com/articles/more-than-40-of-student-borrowers-arent-making-payments-1459971348>

Andrew Haughwout, Donghoon Lee, Joelle Scally, Wilbert van der Klaauw. "Student Loan Borrowing and Repayment Trends." *Federal Reserve Bank of New York* 16. April. 2015. Web. 18 June. 2016. <https://www.newyorkfed.org/medialibrary/media/newsevents/mediaadvisory/2015/Student-Loan-Press-Briefing-Presentation.pdf>